The Architecture of Paradise

The Architecture of Paradise

Survivals of Eden and Jerusalem

WILLIAM ALEXANDER McCLUNG

University of California Press   Berkeley   Los Angeles   London

University of California Press
Berkeley and Los Angeles, California
University of California Press, Ltd.
London, England
© 1983 by
The Regents of the University of
California

Library of Congress Cataloging in
Publication Data

McClung, William A.
The architecture of paradise.
Includes index.
1. Paradise in literature.   2. Architecture
and literature.   I. Title.
PN56.P25M3   809'.93372   81-24071
ISBN 0-520-04587-4   AACR2
Printed in the United States of America

1   2   3   4   5   6   7   8   9

Publication of this book was assisted by
grants from the Hyder Edward Rollins
Fund, Harvard University, and from the
Office of Graduate Studies and Research
and the Department of English, Mississippi
State University.

The quotation from *Utopia* that appears
with figs. 55 and 56 is by kind permission
of Hendricks House, Publishers, New
York.

For my mother

CONTENTS

List of Illustrations   *ix*

Preface   *xiii*

Introduction   *1*

ONE: Eden and Jerusalem   *9*

TWO: Poet and Architect   *47*
Ideal and Epic Architecture   *54*
Morphologies of the Holy City   *70*
The Surface of Things   *82*
Proportionable Rapture   *93*

THREE: Garden and City   *101*
Two Paradises   *101*
Primitive Huts   *114*
Natural Artifacts   *116*
The Rehabilitation of Luxury   *119*
Machines for Living   *130*

Epilogue   *145*

CONTENTS

Notes   *149*

Acknowledgments for Illustrations   *175*

Index   *177*

ILLUSTRATIONS

1. Limbourg brothers, "The Story of Adam
   and Eve," early fifteenth century 4
2. Lucas Cranach(?), illustration for Genesis, 1534 5
3. Hieronymus Bosch, "The Garden of Eden," ca. 1500 6
4. View of Nauvoo, Illinois, from an 1857 drawing 10
5. Nauvoo Temple, ca. 1847 11
6. God as architect of the universe, from the
   medieval *Bible Moralisée* 12
7. St. Augustine, Rome and the celestial city,
   from a fifteenth-century edition of
   De Civitate Dei 21
8. Frontispiece to Henry Hawkins's
   Partheneia Sacra, 1633 22
9. Detail from the plan of the monastery
   of St. Gall, ca. 820 23
10. Jerusalem as "navel of the world," from a
    sixteenth-century map 28
11. Plan of the Temple of Jerusalem, 1632 29
12. Christ in glory, apse, Santa Pudenziana,
    Rome, ca. 400 32
13. Martyrs in bliss, apse, Hagios Georgios,
    Thessaloniki, ca. 355 33
14. Detail from Alonso Cano,
    Vision of St. John, 1635–1637 36
15. Lucas Cranach(?), illustration for
    Revelation, 1534 37
16. Lucas Cranach, *The Golden Age*, ca. 1530 42

17. The Garden of Love in the *Roman de la Rose*,
late fifteenth-century manuscript 43

18. Jacob Judah Leon, drawing of the
Temple mount, 1642 55

19. George Wither, the figure of the perfect man, 1635 56

20. Vitruvius's ideal city, 1521 57

21. Filarete, plan of Sforzindo, 1470 58

22. After Buonaiuto Lorini,
plan of an ideal city, 1592 59

23. After Vincenzo Scamozzi, plan of
an ideal city, 1615 59

24. Francesco di Giorgio, an ideal city, ca. 1470 60

25. Bernard Lamy, the tabernacle in the desert, 1720 66

26. Theodore Busink, reconstruction of the
Temple of Solomon, 1970 67

27. Anonymous woodcut representing
Jerusalem, 1593 73

28. Giovanni Paolo Panini, painting of the interior
of the Pantheon in Rome, eighteenth century 76

29. George Sandys, engraving of Constantinople, 1621 80

30. Chevalier Fossatti, engraving of the interior
of Hagia Sophia, 1852 81

31 and 32. Juan Bautista Villalpando, front and side
elevations of the Temple of Solomon, 1604 84–85

33 and 34. Bernard Lamy, plan and general view of
the Temple of Jerusalem, 1720 86–87

35. Johann Fischer von Erlach, general view of the
Temple mount, 1725 88

36. Juan Bautista Villalpando, interior of the
Holy of Holies, 1604 89

37. William Weeks, preliminary design for
Nauvoo temple, mid-1840s 90

38. Sun capital from the executed Nauvoo temple, ca. 1847 . . 91

39. Filarete, illustration of primitive construction, 1470 94

40. Jean Goujon, illustration of primitive
 construction, 1547 95

41 and 42. Illustrations of prototypical
 architecture, 1547 and 1673 96–97

43. Inigo Jones, drawing for the palace of
 Oceanus, 1624 99

44. Detail from Fra Angelico, *The Last Judgment*,
 ca. 1430 102

45 and 46. William Blake, "Adam and Eve Sleeping"
 and "Raphael Conversing with
 Adam and Eve," ca. 1808 112–113

47. George Wither, a tortoise and a country
 cottage, 1635 117

48. Marc-Antoine Laugier, the goddess
 Architectura, 1755 120

49. Maison Carrée, ca. 20–15 B.C., engraving
 by Charles-Louis Clérisseau 121

50. Eugène Emmanuel Viollet-Le-Duc, illustration
 of the first hut, 1876 122

51 and 52. Sir James Hall, illustrations of
 Gothic architecture, 1813 124–125

53. Sketch of the Walden pond hut, 1854 127

54. Le Corbusier, *Une ville contemporaine* project, 1922 134

55 and 56. Le Corbusier, *Plan Voisin* project, 1925 136–137

57. Le Corbusier, *ville radieuse* project, 1930s 138

58 and 59. Frank Lloyd Wright, Broadacre City project,
 1934–1958: landscape and plan 140–141

60. Frank Lloyd Wright, quadruple
 housing project, 1900 142

61. Lúcio Costa and Oscar Niemeyer,
 Brasília, 1956–1960: the mall 146

62. Studio Archizoom Associati, "No-Stop City:
 A Climatic Universal City," 1970 147

In *Literary Architecture: Essays Toward a Tradition*, Ellen Eve Frank refers to "the condition of harmony, that architecture be natural and nature be architectural."[1] Her own harmonies are those of the Victorians and early modern masters she celebrates—Pater, Hopkins, Proust, and James—but her adroit formula, which I have lifted from its context, goes far toward defining the harmonies that are the object of the present work. Like her, I am interested in the middle ground of the imagination that both "reads" and "informs" (or "gives form to") architecture and literature alike, extending and dissolving what is solid in the continuum of a prolonged idea and bodying forth what is immaterial through the verbal representation of enduring structures. To find that middle ground, I have gone to what seem to me to be the roots of the matter, the paradigmatic structured and literary paradises of Eden and Jerusalem.

In examining architecture and literature as interinanimating arts, Frank has helped give shape to a discipline of thought only occasionally active in earlier criticism. Comparisons between the arts, especially between literature and painting, are of course many and venerable, yet claims made for the parallelism or analogies of one art to another have rarely satisfied the skeptical. Norris Kelly Smith's study of Frank Lloyd Wright is a rare example of a critical intelligence capable of defining, on one side of the coin, the presence of metaphor and "content" in architectural forms.[2] Frank's study, though grounded in literary rather than architectural history, goes beyond its profound analysis of architectural imagery as a shaping or informing principle in literature to lay the groundwork for a methodology of *ut architectura poesis* and *ut poesis architectura*. It is to this kind of examination of architecture and language as not only correlative but reciprocal phenomena that I direct this book.

In 1977 Michael Mooney asked me to read a paper for a special session he was to chair at that year's Modern Language Association convention in Chicago. The session was devoted to "Iconographic Representations of 'The Earthly Paradise,'" and my initial thanks must go to him and to John Perlette for launching this enterprise. At a much later date Stephen Orgel, Kenneth Bleeth, and Ronald Murray did me the honor of reading the manuscript that grew out of that initial exercise in literary iconography, and I shall always be indebted to their patience and perceptivity. Since the matter passed into the hands of the University of California Press, I have been fortunate to have the unfailing intelligence and skill of my editor and namesake, William J. McClung, and of Marilyn Schwartz and Estelle Jelinek. For the typing of the manuscript itself, no easy task, I wish to thank Kendra Crenshaw.

Portions of Chapter 3 have appeared in a different context in my "The Matter of Metaphor: Literary Myths of Construction," *Journal of the Society of Architectural Historians*, 40, no. 4 (December 1981). I am grateful to the editor, Naomi Miller, for giving me the opportunity to rethink portions of the present work in the light of that undertaking.

INTRODUCTION

Mankind has lost its dignity, but Art has
recovered it and conserved it in significant
stones.

(SCHILLER,   *On Aesthetic Education*)

Paradise is a strange land but a familiar presence; few have been there,
but many people have an idea of what it is like. As a garden at one end
of time and a city at the other, Paradise is in one sense remote from
worldly concerns. But Eden has not been allowed to rest in memory,
nor Jerusalem to choose its time of arrival. The study of Paradise must
take up not only the two scriptural versions, or models, but their re-
creations in both simple and complex or synthesized forms. These
re-creations exist within the time of human history and the matrices
of human societies, and they consist both of words and of stones; that
is, both literature and architecture have maintained Paradise in our
lives as a real presence. In both media the translations, or re-creations,
are both literal and metaphoric.

Paradise, in all senses of the word, is the most striking place I can
discover where an immaterial vision and a material structure or
system of relationships are brought together and depend upon each
other. That relationship and that dependence exist in literary versions
of Paradise that incorporate to a greater or lesser extent the description of Paradise as a physical entity, whether garden, city, or a
combination of both; and that relationship exists in architecture that

1

pretends to define or enclose heavenly space or to translate to earth the properties of heaven.

The architecture of my title is thus real architecture, whether actually built or existing in literature, and it is the subject of this book to the extent that the relationship of craft to nature is the subject. The translation of the archetypal models of Paradise into various syntheses, literal and metaphoric, verbal and material, provides a frame of reference within which is continued the struggle to define what "nature" is and what behavior is natural for men. The contradiction between garden and city and the complicated kinds of syntheses between them are pointers to the ambiguous moral status of craft as well as efforts to resolve that ambiguity.

At no one point but as a general trend, Paradise ceases to be religious in conception and becomes something else—something that may be political, economic, ethical, or erotic, according to the human capacity or discipline of thought understood to be the key to spiritual and material fulfillment. The search for Paradise is thus an effort to discover the correct relationship between man, nature, and craft; and as a phenomenon both of secular literature and of urban planning and design, "Paradise" devolves into versions of arcadia and utopia, the one an Eden, the other a Jerusalem—to modify Renato Poggioli's compelling formula—without theology.[1] What an unreligious society expects in the way of a perfect or perfected state of being generally requires something from each model. I am only secondarily concerned with formal literary, architectural, and political analyses of either arcadian or utopian modes of thought and action, but I shall try to show the persistence and interrelatedness of the hortulan and urban models of Paradise and to show that two active and intellectual disciplines, literature and architecture, are penetrated by a single, polarized metaphor or metaphorical mode of thought.

The existence of several distinguished and recent studies of Eden makes it unnecessary for me to dwell upon the typological relationship between the first garden and all that have followed. In arguing, however, for the ascendancy of an architecture over a horticulture of Paradise, I shall depart from the paradigms set forth in the work of Stanley Stewart and Terry Comito.[2] Not all but much of ideal or paradisal gardening after Eden is walled, and the walled gardens are their subject; because both *garden* and its Hebrew equivalent *gan* descend from verbs meaning to guard or to protect, all gardens might seem to be walled. But the Yahwist garden of Genesis 2 is not, and the word *paradise*, connoting more specifically an enclosed park,[3] does not occur in its cognate Hebrew form, *pardes*, before Nehemiah 2:8 and was never adopted by the rabbinic texts of the Talmud.[4] In the first century A.D., Philo Judaeus wrote of Paradise only that "it is a dense place full of all kinds of trees";[5] "a grove" (ἄλσος), echoes St. Gregory of Nyssa in the fourth century, "planted with leafy trees";[6] "a most beautiful place in the East, in which [were] trees of various kinds" is the simple formula in the twelfth-century *Elucidarium* of Honorius of Autun.[7]

Exegetical tradition, however, tended eventually to assimilate the distinctive but unenclosed garden of Genesis to the enclosed one of Canticles (Song of Solomon) and both to the walled city of Revelation. Stanley Stewart's pursuit of a secret garden that manifested itself across centuries of art and literature refers us to the important archetype generated from this conflation but not to the first garden itself, which was no secret—as Satan discovers when Uriel readily directs him to Eden in *Paradise Lost* (III, 722ff.).[8] John Bunyan noted the vulnerability of the garden of Genesis and cited it to justify the fact that the Paradise to come is urban:

Adam, you know, was once so rich and wealthy, that he had the garden of Eden, the paradise of pleasure, yea, and also the whole world to boot, for his inheritance; but mark, in all his glory he was without a wall; wherefore presently, even at the very first assault of the adversary, he was not only worsted as touching his person and standing, but even stripped of all his treasure, his paradise taken from him. . . .[9]

1

Eden with walls and interior architecture,
from Pol, Jan, and Herman Limbourg,
Les Très Riches Heures du Duc de Berry, early
fifteenth century.

2

Eden without walls, coterminous with a
continent, in a Lucas Cranach(?) illustration for Genesis in Martin Luther's
German Bible, 1534.

3

Eden without walls, as a slice of landscape,
in Hieronymus Bosch's synoptic
representation from *The Last Judgment*, left
panel, ca. 1500.

Pastoral societies are conspicuously vulnerable; strangers penetrate the arcadia of Sidney's romance, and brigands ravage the arcadians of Book VI of *The Faerie Queene*. By contrast, utopian visions typically ensure security through elaborate fortifications or safe distancing. The presence of a wall of some kind, artificial or natural, around the actual and metaphorical gardens of literature and around the medieval claustral space and the Renaissance plot is the primary architectural event that marks a synthesis between Eden and its rival archetype. In tracing the relationships of opposition and accommodation between garden and city, we shall consequently find compromised Edens, paradisal gardens to some degree assimilated to architectural phenomena like walls, temples, or cities. In instances where the garden must dominate, the iconography of Paradise is of a special kind, one that constitutes a definition of the proper relationship of craft to nature; here architecture is accommodated when it submits to perceived laws of nature or laws of the nature of materials of construction, or insofar as it may be identified with the lives of virtuous inhabitants. This manner of construction and the ethical tradition of hostility to material display and to craft make up one of the two governing conceptions of paradisal or ideal architecture; in conjunction with the opposing model, of building distinguished by richness of surface and sophistication of form, this conception will lead us through literary and theoretical versions of Paradise, arcadia, and utopia to the modern linkage of secular virtue with city planning in its large sense, the sense of Frank Lloyd Wright's Broadacre City and of Le Corbusier's *ville radieuse*.

A recent inquiry into the scientific and utopian assumptions of modern architecture notes that "the ecstatic component of modern architecture has received a comparatively insufficient attention."[10] The ecstatic component in building, which descends mainly from the idea of a heavenly city and from the attribution to architecture of heavenly properties, is my subject. Like *Collage City* by Colin Rowe and Fred Koetter, my study is syncretistic and cannot pretend to touch every base in literature and architecture or in the related areas of moral philosophy that define the relationship of nature, man, and craft. The line or chain of transmission from mythic to metaphorical models of Paradise is neither single nor direct; more familiar in the examination of the sources of modern architecture and more clearly documented is a pattern of romantic scientific/utopian thought. It is my belief that the wide range of the present study, though diffusing the pedigree of modern architecture through many areas of inquiry and achievement, will contribute to an understanding of its ultimate source.

ONE

Eden and Jerusalem

Haf ȝe no woneȝ in castel-walle,
Ne maner þer ȝe may mete & won?
Þou telleȝ me of Jerusalem, the ryche ryalle,
Þer Dauid dere watȝ dyȝt on trone;
Bot by þyse holteȝ hit con not hone. . . .

(*Pearl*)

Between 1841 and 1846 the Mormon community of Nauvoo, Illinois,
dwelled in a zoned town asymmetrically partitioned into sacred and
secular areas. The former was made up of two noncontiguous buildings: the temple and the residence of the prophet Joseph Smith,
whose earlier "Plat of the City of Zion" served as the basis of the new
town's plan. Both buildings were distinguished by their conspicuous
sites, great mass, relative complexity of plan, and—in the case of the
temple—elaborate ornamentation of the facades. The temple easily
dominated the riverfront town. The other zone was laid out as a
garden-city of solid brick residences, no more than four to a block,
each occupying a corner and backed by extensive gardens.

The rhetoric of the community was overtly paradisal in nature and
reflected the division. Smith cast his instructions for the building of
the temple (the plan of which, like that of the "plat," he said God sent
to him) in ersatz King James English, loosely but frequently echoing
John of Patmos's vision of the New Jerusalem, whereas a local

4

General view of Nauvoo, Illinois, drawing
from Henry Lewis, *Das Illustrierte
Mississippi*, Düsseldorf, 1857.

5

Nauvoo Temple, from an old
daguerreotype, ca. 1847.

6

A metaphor taken literally: God as
architect of the universe, from the
anonymous medieval illuminated
manuscript the *Bible Moralisée*.

editorial of 1842 exhorted the citizens in plain but eloquent language to marry their houses to their gardens:

Let the division fences be lined with peach and mulberry trees . . . and the houses surrounded with roses and prairie flowers, and their porches covered with grapevines, and we shall soon have some idea of how Eden looked.[1]

The town, of course, was not a success partly because commerce, banned from the sacred city (except that the prophet's residence was to double as a pilgrimage hostel), could find no convenient focal point in the low-density residential quarter. The assassination of Joseph Smith and the subsequent exile to Deseret aborted whatever accommodations the citizens might have been able to make, and the Eden/Jerusalem dichotomy was enforced at Salt Lake City with far less rigor.

The significance of this remarkably literal experiment in the construction of Paradise is not, however, primarily economic but mythic and metaphoric: mythic because Nauvoo is a striking instance of the duality of the Paradise tradition, metaphoric because the paradisal myth informs the planning and architecture of other communities in ways that are no less significant for the absence of theology. In his sacred structures, Smith utilized the uniquely architectural phenomena of massing, groundplan, and ornamentation of facades to express the importance of the house of God, the threshold of the Paradise to come.[2] In the residential quarter, he metaphorically reconstituted Paradise lost, the garden that was man's proper environment on this planet and that continues to serve as the model even after nature, like man, has fallen. Yet Smith's version of Eden is compromised, as his Jerusalem is not, by an architectural presence whose very modesty and degree of integration with nature—with the gardens that grow around and even into the house—are evidence that Eden in its pure form is irrecoverable. The terms in which the antitypes of the celestial city manifest themselves at Nauvoo are wholly architectural, but the terrestrial paradise must accommodate the lapsarian fact of the need for shelter. The architecture of Paradise is thus dual, as is Paradise itself: an architecture of heaven is juxtaposed to an architecture of nature.

The paradises between which the iron age of history is a parenthesis are a garden without a building and a building enclosing a garden. One, conspicuously unprotected, is lost or displaced beyond reach; the other, a fortress, is accessible only at the apocalypse. Both are dwelling places for the body as well as the spirit, and in recommending themselves to us as models, they propose different kinds of bliss, physical and spiritual. The backward-looking Edenic vision is arcadian and admits the crafts, if at all, only on peculiar and constricting conditions; the impulse that looks forward to a city is utopian and glorifies the craft of which God is a patron, intolerant of a state of existence that, in Thomas Hobbes's contemptuous phrase, has "no commodious building."[3]

The quest for Eden is characteristically bodied forth in the negative tropes of the golden age, such as the absence of war or of seafaring, of mining, of bad weather, of women, and/or of a sense of shame. One of the tropes, motives, or topoi is the city or architecture in the mere form of a simple house. Even in georgic literature, which celebrates farming and in which the crafts appropriate to agriculture must be tolerated, "building" is justified only by being identified with the relatively pristine lives of the in-dwellers and often (an important corollary) by being identified with natural materials of construction or with methods of construction understood to be natural.

The celestial city, by contrast, is localized among us in sacred urban enclosures, primarily the temple and the palace, within whose highly wrought premises we fulfill our capacities for craft and art, finding the completion in ritual and worship of our capacity for politics, that is, the life of men in cities. The wholly natural structures of the

garden, as well as the architecture assimilated to its state of naturalness and thereby neutralized, exert a cool, diffuse influence, the contrary of the electric stimulation brought about by phenomena that in
combination are peculiar to architecture: great mass, splendor or brilliance of surface, symbolic or ideal proportions, complexity of plan,
and reiteration or multiplication of parts. The distinction between the
Paradise of serenity and the Paradise of ecstasy is historical and arises
in pre-Christian apocalyptic literature; the emotional climate peculiar
to the "new" Jerusalem is specified in the earliest recorded use of the
term, in the Testament of Dan (5:12) of ca. 106 B.C.: "And the saints
shall rest in Eden, And in the New Jerusalem shall the righteous
rejoice." If the garden where even God did not disdain to enjoy the
cool of the day invites repose, so, according to Revelation, the city
compels celebration:

And the building of the wall of it was jasper: and the city was pure
gold, like unto clear glass. And the foundations of the wall of the city
were garnished with all manner of precious stones. . . . And the twelve
gates were twelve pearls; every several gate was of one pearl: and the
street of the city was of pure gold, as it were transparent glass.

$$(21:19-21)^4$$

Medieval theologians in the tradition of St. Augustine, accus-
tomed to multiple readings of Scripture, would understand in this
description not only *allegoria quid intellegendum* ("allegory: what is to
be understood") (that is, holy church) but also *anagoge* (ἀναγωγή)
quid appetendum ("anagogy: what is to be sought"), a sensuous
anticipation of the life to come.[5] Mass and richness trigger our immediate enthusiasm while the ideal cubic proportions as well as the
paradoxical transparence of the luminous materials of wall and street
invite a subtler appreciation. These are the prototypical constituents
of an architecture of heaven and, when abstracted from an actual
building, may be understood as the phenomena that serve to sanctify

that building. Here we anticipate no activity like that of Adam, who in *Paradise Lost* pursues the one acceptable craft of gardening. The shortcomings will be apparent to anyone who has seen heaven in a wild flower, but the poverty of greenery in the golden cube should disturb us no more than the structural vacancies of the primal garden. True Paradise may be Paradise lost, as Proust observed, but he noted also that "le souvenir d'une certaine image n'est que le regret d'un certain instant"[6] – thereby deepening Quintilian's dry recommendation of architecture as an *aide-mémoire*.[7] Proust's axiom is useful in reverse: sorrow for a lost time is sorrow for a lost place, an "image" intimately associated with a structure, an enclosure, or a dwelling of some kind. *Nulli certa domus* ("no private homes"), Virgil wrote of the Elysian Fields,[8] but "no fixed abode," the language of the police blotter, better conveys the anxiety of houselessness. Eden ought to be the place where it is not possible to lose one's way,[9] but the unpathed, unstructured wood is for Gaston Bachelard the primal dystopia: in it we are lost and, therefore, trapped and enclosed, but vulnerable because the unstructured space is infinitely penetrable.[10]

Hyle, Aristotle's term for the chaos that is informed by *nous*, or mind, literally means "forest"; so Virgil as glossed by Servius in the late fourth century signifies by *silva* a psychic realm of violent and primitive passions.[11] Arguably, the phenomenology of the postlapsarian forest – what Adam proleptically terms "these wild woods forlorn" (*Paradise Lost*, IX, 910) – need not color an analysis of unfallen nature, but it must govern efforts to reconstruct a garden that will compensate for the millennia of lost time. That garden must offer a security to neutralize the consciousness of vulnerability. Milton's bower in *Paradise Lost* corresponds to Bachelard's description of the house as symbol and embodiment of virtues like love, intimacy, and protectiveness,[12] the place where memory and dream are fulfilled in the atemporality of concretized space. Here, in a structure, time is gathered up, arrested, and preserved, as John Ruskin understood in drawing an analogy with literature:

There are but two strong conquerors of the forgetfulness of men, Poetry and Architecture; and the latter in some sort includes the former, and is mightier in its reality; it is well to have, not only what men have thought and felt, but what their hands have handled, and their strength wrought, and their eyes beheld, all the days of their life.[13]

In the *City of God*, XXII, 30, St. Augustine distinguishes between the Edenic and the resurrected state as *posse non mori*, "ability not to die," and *non posse mori*, "impossibility of dying." The iconology of organic and inorganic paradises bears out the fragility of the former condition and the security of the latter.

The history of Eden as a model for the state of bliss is a mixed one, marked by an early and irreversible loss and maintained by compromises made in the structure of the original model to accommodate it to the condition of a saved rather than an unfallen race. A confusion, never resolved among either apocalyptic Jewish or early Christian writers, lay in the distinctions between the lost terrestrial garden, a place of final beatitude that might be either Eden or a New Eden, and a surviving terrestrial garden-paradise, the existence of which might be inferred from the belief that it was destined to be the Paradise at the end of time.[14] Ezra (36:35; cf. Isaiah 51:3) identified the Paradise to come as Eden, but the equation did not survive pre-Christian apocalyptic writings. What rabbinic texts of the Talmud (sixty-three tractates written over the millennium preceding the fifth and sixth centuries A.D.) termed "Days of the Messiah" and "World to Come" were never consistently defined either in nature or time of occurrence, nor was there any consensus on the relationship of the "World to Come" with Eden. Occasionally, the notion of a "Future to Come" (*le-atid lavo*) embraces both a renewed earth and "heaven" in some sense.[15]

The uncertain position of Eden in space and time was heightened by evolving conceptions of the physical properties of Paradise and of its way of life. Eden sinks beneath the formidable vision of the blessed, scholars all, studying the Talmud in Paradise;[16] the waning of a pastoral vision of communality in nature is evident in the *Midrash Konen*, where the just are classified and separately housed.[17] As a corollary to such sophisticated revisions of the paradisal state, the "garden" is first decorated with and then overwhelmed by material imagery. Golden canopies and tables for the feast and rest of the blessed[18] lead to the *Gan Eden* of the *Midrash Konen*, a building of five rooms fashioned of rare woods and precious metals.[19] In Ezekiel 28:13, "the garden of God" is a jeweler's emporium.

The problems of transposing the model of Eden to the other end of history are many, and they turn principally upon memory; Eden cannot be new, and to regain it as it was is only to acknowledge the failure of history. For better or for worse—and the Christian conception of the *felix culpa* that is generally acknowledged to be central, for example, to *Paradise Lost* urges us always to choose the better—the experience of the knowledge of good and evil entails a progressive notion of existence in time; the stasis that lies at the end of the progression must be Paradise but not the same Paradise from which knowledge of good and evil was excluded.

Eden might retain a serious role in the drama at the end of history: there Messiah would lift the curse from Adam (Testament of Levi 18:10–11), but the arcadian components are irrelevant, and the role is formal. This Eden is, in any case, already subordinated to the heaven of heavens; it is essentially the "third heaven," a provisional paradise where by tradition the just awaited resurrection, with Enoch and Elijah, perhaps with the thief to whom Christ promised Paradise "this day" (Luke 23:43) and, according to Origen and others, with martyrs, virgins, even all the righteous in Christ.[20] St. Augustine, who denied that the garden would be restored on earth,[21] while admitting the "third heaven,"[22] supplanted the occasional Jewish eschatological garden (as in 1 Enoch 32:3–6) with his "City of God," which ensured the perpetuation of John of Patmos's vision.

As a general pattern it may be said that to the extent that Paradise is of the past, it is arcadian and open, the epitome of that nature of which it is a small part; to the extent that it is imagined to survive into the present (but in some obscure or inaccessible or forbidden spot), it is a secret garden walled or otherwise barred against man; to the extent that Paradise signifies the Paradise to come, it is urban and conspicuously fortified. *Garden* in the New Testament is merely and always κῆπος, never παράδεισος[23] (Luke 13:19; Timothy 18:1, 26 and 19:41). The history of Paradise is thus the history of the loss of belief in the possibility of pastoral, that is, of unelaborated nature benign without reservation, limitation, or threat. The uncertain status of the garden in history reflects the failure of an arcadian or pastoral model of beatific existence within the context of a purged and renewed heaven and earth; the survival of Eden depends, therefore, upon whatever accommodation can be reached with the city. To survive, in fact, Eden must become a garden-city.

The first significant synthesis was Ezekiel's, who in a time of catastrophe saw Israel in a vision restored in the form of an immense temple, excruciatingly precise in proportions; out of it issued a river that proceeded to fertilize a dead land (Ezekiel 47). The ultimate topical descendant in the Bible of this garden-city is the New Jerusalem, to which Eden gains admittance in the shrunken and symbolical form of the water and the tree of life (Revelation 22). Their presence is essentially tropological, as Bunyan appreciates: "Oh, they will be green, savoury, reviving, flourishing, growing Christians, that shall walk the street of New Jerusalem."[24] Yet a significant inversion has occurred: now garden is *enclosed* by city.

The garden that had in fact established itself as the typological forerunner of the celestial tree and water of life was no longer that of Genesis but of Canticles, to which in painting and literature a tree was conventionally added (without scriptural authority), and the fountain of which bodied forth the ambiguous suggestion of such in Genesis 2:6, 10.[25] In its assimilation to the enclosed garden of Solomon, the Yahwist *hortus* lost its implicit quality of exposure to become a defensible paradise, to be identified not with the Eden of Adam and Eve but with the Eden mysteriously surviving and waiting for the Paradise to come—where, at the end of history, it completes its withdrawal behind a wall in ultimate abbreviation and confinement as the botanical garden of the golden city. In Christian typology the paradise-garden of Canticles was understood to figure many things, such as the body of Mary:

> that garden [sc. Eden] far, exceeding sundry wayes,
> As perfect second woorkes, exceed things wrought before.
> All closely wall'd about, inviolately stayes,
> No serpent can get in. . . .[26]

The significance of the wall as the primary architectural event has been neatly expressed by Robert Venturi: the wall contradicts the flow of exterior space, yet it is a complex element that at the point of transition resolves the discordancy between open and closed spaces.[27] Within the context of Christian symbolism, the wall of Paradise signifies divine intervention, a redemptive interruption of the natural order, "pointing up the power of Grace to undo the natural propensities of human will [and signifying] life-giving separation between nature and Grace."[28]

Not only the walls but the interior architecture of the *hortus conclusus* might refer to the displacement of the law by grace. The frontispiece to Henry Hawkins's *Partheneia Sacra* of 1633 juxtaposes a ruinous castle (representing the Temple of Jerusalem) to an elaborate Renaissance structure within a walled garden; thus, both in its protective walling and in its incorporation of architectural imagery, the paradise-garden is loosed from Edenic and arcadian moorings and assimilated to the city of God. Nature as redeemed and as agent of redemption cannot now be the nature known before the Fall:

7

Type and antitype: St. Augustine, in
Rome, envisioning the celestial city,
from Niccolo Polani's fifteenth-century
edition of *De Civitate Dei*.

8

"Far exceeding Eden, all closely walled
about," the garden becomes a dynamic and
synchronic figure, fusing the lost paradise
with the one to come, in the frontispiece
to Henry Hawkins's *Partheneia Sacra*, 1633.

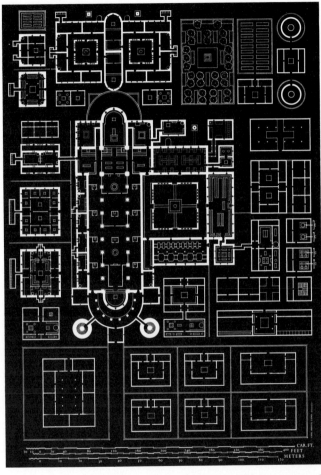

9

The foursquare cloister garden lies at the
center of the compound of the ideal
monastery of St. Gall, from the original
Plan of St. Gall, ca. 820.

typically nature comes to reproduce the structures and operations of
the Church, even to the point, in Henry Vaughan's seventeenth-cen-
tury poem "Regeneration," of physically mimicking the forms of
ecclesiastical architecture and ritual.[29] Paradise on earth after the Fall
is always provisional; enclosed by natural and artificial barriers, it
expresses through its iconography the present disjunction between
nature and grace and through its phenomenology the difference
between open and enclosed space.

The Yahwist garden is, besides, inherently unstable, penetrated
by visits from above and lying over a flux of waters below—and so
U. Milo Kaufmann has argued, locating in the seventeenth century
the displacement, in literature and painting, of enclosed gardens by
open landscapes, whose capacity for change is inherent.[30] The claustral garden, by contrast, where it is strictly an image of Paradise
rather than a metaphor for it, should be seen as such only within
a rather narrow context. The foursquareness and hydraulics of the
medieval cathedral and monastic cloisters are conventionally understood as Edenic in nature and reference, but the more congruent
model is the celestial Jerusalem, which is in like manner foursquare,
planted, and irrigated. Clearly, the cloister garden of the ideal monastery of St. Gall, and of many others, is a synthesis of hortulan
and urban elements, but which should be thought of as primary
and which as assimilated to the other?

Arguably, when one is perceived as the figure, the other becomes
the ground, and vice versa without resolution. But although many
(like Andrew Marvell's "Mower Against Gardens") have felt that
nature is compromised by artifice, I know of no objection to architecture adorned by a garden. As an image of Eden, the claustral garden
at every point (in its walls, its paths, its fountains and urns) reminds
us that Eden survives by compromise with a fallen world, as a fortress.
As an equivalent of Jerusalem, it is a city that has acquired a garden—the garden whose natural properties, like the bodies of the resurrected dead, are apotheosized by incorporation into the "artifice of

eternity." Viewed from this angle, the claustral garden is anticipatory and celebratory rather than memorial and ironic.[31]

Yet the neatest exposition of the cloister's paradisal rhetoric is Joachim of Fiore's in the late twelfth century. The cloister does prefigure the Paradise to come, which is, however, the renewed earthly paradise of the millennium, which he sees as a utopia of monks.[32] This is only a prelude to heaven, a specific kind of enclosed space, the meaning of which lies in the yoking together of contraries and the appropriateness of which, in both postlapsarian and millennial terms, is earthly rather than heavenly.

Heavenly space is different. In its terrestrial origin it develops upon a site that is understood in some way to be set apart from undifferentiated nature and proximate to heaven, connected by a mountain, a tree, or a vine.[33] As τέμενος, from which templum is derived, suggests, the site is at first neither garden nor building but a hallowed spot that may be a grove.[34] As the preeminent nexus of earth and heaven, a mountain transfers its prestige to the architectural phenomena—temples to honor or to house the god—that crown it; by extension, the surrounding city acquires sanctity. Zion, thought to be only eighteen miles from heaven,[35] is a city as well as a site, typically understood in synecdoche by the architectural feature through which the deity entered and left: "On the holy mount stands the city he founded; the Lord loves the gates of Zion more than all the dwelling places of Jacob" (Psalm 87). Babylon is literally the gate of the gods, Bab-ilani,[36] and as early as 2000 B.C. the common architectural properties of Middle Eastern mythology appear in a dream granted to the priest-king Gudea of Lagash, whom a Sumerian poem records as having been thus shown the plan of a temple and ordered to build it.[37] The divine sanction is of course repeated in God's instructions to Moses to build the tabernacle (Exodus 25–27), the first of the houses he says he will live in.

Thus, the historical Jerusalem may claim the role of "the holy city"[38] of the prophets (Nehemiah 11:1; Isaiah 48:2 and 52:10) or "the world's navel" (Ezekiel 5:5). "Beautiful for situation, the joy of the whole earth, is mount Zion . . . God is known in her palaces for a refuge," the psalmist sings; "walk about Zion, and go round about her: tell the towers thereof. Mark ye well her bulwarks, consider her palaces" (Psalm 48). The sanctity of the city centers in one structure, the Temple, where the deity "who builds his chambers in heaven" has elected "to found his vault upon earth" (Amos 9:9). Still to some extent a local god, the god of a place rather than the Lord of heaven, the Jehovah of 1 Kings requires a residence essentially domestic in design, echoing the plans of Phoenician and other Middle Eastern temples conceived as divine dwellings.[39] Rabbinical tradition attributed to the Temple the power of stabilizing the shaky foundations of the globe and of renewing, through sacrifices performed within it, the fertility of Israel.[40] Subsequent centuries of commentary have imagined the Temple as a microcosm of the world[41] or as a living creature sheltering trees of "vegetable gold," perpetually in fruit[42]–a tradition surviving in Islamic legend and art and visible in the jeweled trees and fruit that decorate the Dome of the Rock.[43] Commonly, the Temple allegorizes the cosmos, as in Josephus[44] or, seventeen centuries later, Joseph Mede, whose *Clavis Apocalyptica* of 1632 analyzes the plan in part: the inner court "signifies the primitive state of the Christian Church," the outer court "signifies the holy City of God"; and so on.[45] The poet Ephraem Syrus (ca. A.D. 306–373) held that the three sections of the Temple corresponded to the three paradises;[46] both hortulan and urban topographies are thus symbolically comprehended within an architectural framework.

The occasion of the destruction of the Temple by the Babylonians in 586 B.C. led Ezekiel to rationalize God's apparent abandonment of his holy city by reconstituting his divine throne as a chariot (Ezekiel 10) and therefore movable. Jehovah's departure is the beginning of the end of Jerusalem's unique historical role, and a Talmudic description of the event suggests the finality of a removal "from ark-cover to cherub, and thence to the threshold, to the court, to the altar, to the roof, to the wall, to the town, to the mountain, to the wilderness, to heaven."[47] What remains is the Temple of Ezekiel's vision, an immaterial prototype unaffected by the ruin of what may now be understood to have been a terrestrial facsimile. God had twice before emphasized to Moses that the tabernacle must conform in design to the pattern revealed to him on the mount (Exodus 25:9, 40); it was a short step to conceive of it as actually erected in heaven.[48] Serving as a model for subsequent earthly temples, the heavenly one gradually was acknowledged as preexistent and predominant, especially when it was compared with the inferior structure completed in Jerusalem in 516 B.C., a big disappointment to the few who remembered its predecessor.[49]

Conquest had shown that the sanctity of the earthly city was provisional, and the succession of political renewals and catastrophes that ended with the sack of Jerusalem by the Romans in A.D. 70 favored both a projection of a restored terrestrial paradise around Mt. Moriah and an emphasis on the permanence of its celestial prototype. As late as the twelfth century A.D., Maimonides follows Jewish apocalyptic tradition in anticipating a revivified earthly city;[50] the prophecy of Isaiah 54:11-12 is an authorization: "I will lay thy stones with fair colors, and lay thy foundations with sapphires. And I will make thy windows of agates, and thy gates of carbuncles, and all thy borders of precious stones." The "new" Jerusalem is more distinctly adumbrated about 166 B.C.,[51] or even before,[52] and first so called about 106 B.C. in the Testament of Dan; but it is revealed to the prophet Baruch after the Roman sack not as a restored earthly city but as a heavenly one—the one, God explains, that always was the city graven upon the palms of his hands (Isaiah 49:16). This celestial city or building (Baruch uses both terms) was, in God's words, "prepared beforehand here from the time when I took counsel to make Paradise, and [I] showed it to Adam before he sinned, but when he transgressed the commandment it was removed from him, as also Paradise," which, like the city, survives in heaven (2 Baruch 4:2-7). Both shall

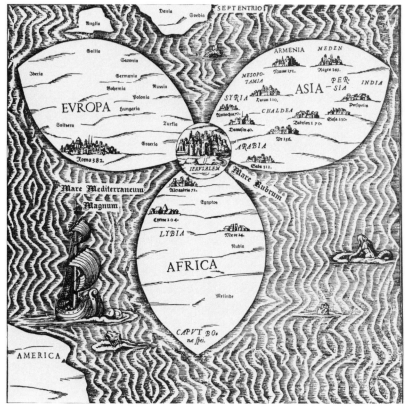

10

"The world's navel," Jerusalem, from a
sixteenth-century map.

Pars II. *IN* BIBΛAPIΔION.   127

cessit, loco Relativi repetitur, aut ejus synonymum
Relativi vice substituitur. Posterioris modi exem-
plum hîc habes, & Act.25.21. Et sanè quid aliud
esse dicemus *Gentibus dari*, hoc est, occupandi po-
testatem fieri, quàm *calcari*? & quid tandem calca-
rent Gentes, nisi id quod eis datum fuerat? ut
hæ quoque voces, non minùs quàm *Atrii* & *Civita-
tis sanctæ*, sese mutuò explicare videantur.

Ad CAP.II.

¶ Ichnographia ΤΟΥ 'ΙΕΡΟΥ, id est,
Templi & Atriorum ejus.

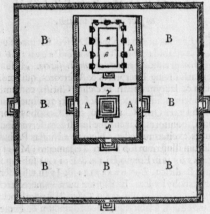

AAAA
*Atrium in-
terius.*
BBBB
BBB
*Atrium ex-
terius.*
  α β
'Ο ΝΑΟΣ
sive Templū.
α *Sanctum
Sanctorum.*
β *Sanctum.*
γ δ *Altare
holocausti.*
Α γ Α δ
*Thysiaste-
rium.*

Duobus hisce Atriis (quorum, & non plurium
Scriptura meminit)posterioribus seculis,in Templo
nimirum

11

Solomon's Temple as a Christian code, the
various courts denoting stages in the
evolution of the Church, from Joseph
Mede, *Clavis Apocalyptica*, 1632.

be revealed (4 Ezra 7:26) and both enjoyed by the blessed (4 Ezra 8:52); the city of David is the offspring of the celestial "Sion, whom thou beholdest as a builded city" (4 Ezra 10:44–45), and in the guise of allegory the prophet witnesses the heavenly city weeping, in the form of a mother, over her ruined earthly child.[53]

The New Testament is a record of the supplanting of the earthly Jerusalem by the heavenly and of Christian antagonism to the vision of a political millenium in Israel.[54] Although Jesus calls the Temple "the house of God" (Matthew 12:4), he foretells its destruction (Matthew 13:1–2); a new temple will rise, but it is spiritual, not material (Mark 14:58; Ephesians 2:19–22; 1 Peter 1:5). Acts records the disciples' continuing attendance and preaching in the Temple [55] until Stephen's rejection of its authority (Acts 6), although, as Milton notes, "the law of Moses ... was not yet fully abrogated, till the destruction of the Temple."[56] Only the celestial prototype endures and is free (Galatians 4:24–26); it is tabernacle (2 Corinthians 5:15), temple (Revelation 21:22–for the celestial city is altogether temple), and city (Hebrews 11:15, 12:22, and 13:14). Especially it is a polity, "τὸ πολίτευμα ἐν οὐρανοῖς" or commonwealth of Philippians (3:20), whose rituals of amity and celebration are adumbrated in Ephesians (2:19): "συμπολῖται τῶν ἁγίων καὶ οἰκεῖοι τοῦ Θεοῦ," and are ideally duplicated here below (Philippians 2:10). They are well caught in the simple verses of Hildebert of Lavardin (d. 1133):

> in plateis huius urbis
> sociatus piis turbis
> cum Moyse et Elia
> pium cantem Alleluia.

> in the streets of this city
> united with the devout throngs
> let me sing, with Moses and Elijah
> a devout Hallelujah.

Ultimately the formulation is St. Augustine's: *"Nam unde ista Dei civitas . . . si non esset socialis vita sanctorum?"* (*City of God*, XIX, 5), that is, "how could there be a city of God if the life of the blessed were not societal in nature?" Because of their diversity and multitude, the blessed, Bunyan argues in his commentary on the Apocalypse, must be housed in a city.[57]

The long road to the heavenly city has been traced in all periods of Western Christianity, particularly in Bunyan's own seventeenth century—by himself, in *Pilgrim's Progress*, and by poets like Henry Vaughan longing, in "The Retreat," for "That shady city of palm trees." It is to medieval literature, however, that we must turn to find the profoundest understanding of the phenomenology of the movement from exposure to enclosure, from isolation to community, and from nature to architecture. In both the anonymous Middle English poem *Pearl* and in Dante's *Commedia*, the translations are achieved with exquisite precision and discrimination between the states of the earthly garden, the paradisal garden, and the city.

Pearl is the narrative of a grief-stricken man who has lost an incomparable jewel, the pearl of the title, in a garden; in a dream he finds it actually reconstituted in the form of a woman, who is not encrusted but synthesized with pearls. The pearl itself is an anagogical prefiguration of heaven, "spotless, pure and clear, / And round without end and bright of tone, / And common to all who righteous were" (lines 737–39).[58] The encounter takes place in a transfigured landscape, not that of "clot" and "moul" (clay and earth) in which the narrator fell asleep, but of jewels and precious metals. But heightened nature of this kind does not satisfy him, and he asks the question given as the epigraph to this chapter: "Have ye no homes within castle wall, / Nor manor where ye may meet and dwell? / Thou tellest me of Jerusalem, the kingdom royal, / Where David dear was established on throne; / But by these groves it did not stand" (lines 917–21).

12 and 13

The commonwealth in the heavens: Christ
in glory in the apse of Santa Pudenziana,
Rome, ca. 400; and martyrs in bliss in the
celestial city in the apse of Hagios
Georgios, Thessaloniki, ca. 355.
The arched and vaulted public buildings
behind Christ suggest Rome itself, but
the martyrs appear in front of the architecture of a theater set.

He receives the vision of St. John's megastructure, to the complex components of which he pointedly avoids attributing allegorical significance.[59] The city glories in splendor of materials, immensity, and excruciating precision of form. Some sense of the extreme edges of such a paradisal experience can be had from a forerunner of Revelation, the so-called Ethiopic Book of Enoch (second to first centuries B.C.), which defines the eschatological mansion as not only crystalline but icy and fiery at once: "there were no delights of life therein" (Ethiopic Book of Enoch 14:9-10, 13).[60] Inhuman splendors, not to be realized in a garden, are conveyed in language glorifying all that is hard and brilliant. In *Pearl*, as in Revelation, Jerusalem is less forbidding but partakes of these qualities. Both cities are the culmination of a transformational process, and what is loose and implicit in the biblical progression from Genesis to Canticles to Ezekiel to Apocalypse is tightly argued in *Pearl's* mutation of landscape into jewelry and jewelry into architecture.

At the poem's center throughout, the pearl is both the stuff and essence of the celestial kingdom (as city and as state of being), and it is also that celestial property that has the power to transform nature. In searching for it, the dreamer perceives, in veiled or incomplete phenomena, the essential properties shared by the pearl and the city. In his original garden, he is certain that the spot where the pearl lies hidden must be protected from the destructive effects of time and weather (stanza 3);[61] in the jeweled landscape, he learns that what he had lost was in reality not a pearl but a rose—subject to law of "kynde"—and (by implication) that what is perishable, however lovely, is not of the pearl's true nature.

In the city, the identity of the title object is made clear not only by the literally "pearly" gates, which, like the pearl itself, are means of access to Paradise, but also by the structure of Jerusalem. Where rituals of festivity bind the citizens in procession, "It were not fit jewels of such price / Should lie unsheltered by roof or wall" (lines 929-30).[62] Their houses are translucent (lines 1027, 1049-50), re-

peating both the appearance and the enveloping nature of the translucent jewel. Both the city and the transfigured citizens are the pearl,
continuous with each other and with it.

In its identity with the pearl, the city acquires the properties of
luminosity, hardness, and consistency of form and substance from
shell to core that define the unitary experience of bliss. In these at-
tributes the city is distinguished from, and superior to, not only the
landscape of "clot" and "moul" but also that of crystal and beryl,
having an identity of formal properties with substance not possible in
the garden—either the one subject to decay or the jeweled one, where,
in *Pearl* and elsewhere, we must tolerate an epistemological gap
between the precious substances and their theoretically organic
forms. Ultimately, the dreamer sees the pearl both as the glorified
woman of his vision and as the Paradise within which she is glorified,
and with which her pearled body is continuous. Like her (lines 253,
277–78), the lamb is called "jewel" (line 1124) in a moment of ecstasy
that suggests, along with the subsequent rhapsody on his color, the
identity of the pearl with Christ.[63]

The symbol can be stretched no farther; it binds "paradise"
together as the lamb, his city, and his people in a polity to be
understood in terms alien to the perishable rose. The central symbol is
of course jewelry, not architecture, but its qualities are those toward
which celestial architecture strives; the most important of them is
unity, which we understand anagogically through the pearl's cir-
cularity, color, and translucency. Another means to the same end
occurs in Dante.

John Ruskin has memorably contrasted the "fencelessness and
thicket of sin" of the dark wood at the opening of the *Inferno* with the
"fencelessness and thicket of free virtue" of the earthly paradise at the
summit of purgatory.[64] Dante's is the fullest working out of the
medieval sense of the meaning of enclosure, progression to which is
synonymous with fulfillment—regardless of what is being fulfilled.
Both dark wood and garden precede, temporally, psychologically,

14 and 15

Twelve-gated cities, having the literal and
domestic qualities, though not the
translucency, of the heavenly mansions
described in *Pearl*: detail from Alonso
Cano, *Vision of St. John*, 1635–1637; and an
illustration (Lucas Cranach[?]) for
Revelation, in Martin Luther's
German Bible, 1534.

and morally, the final complexly ordered states toward which they tend: "the fettered and fearful order of eternal punishment" and "the loving and constellated order of eternal happiness."[65] The earlier state is immature and temporary, the latter complete and forever. "Qui sarai tu poco tempo silvano," Beatrice tells Dante in the garden: "here for a while you will be a woodsman"; "e sarai meco senza fine cive / di quella Roma onde Cristo e romano" (*Purgatorio*, XXXII, 100–02): "and with me you will forever be a citizen of that Rome where Christ is a Roman."

Beatrice leaves us in no doubt that Dante is going to a city: "Vedi nostra città", she cries (*Paradiso*, XXX, 130), "see our city," whose urbanity is fixed by its identification with the supreme political institution of history. The garden is abandoned, and eventually (*Paradiso*, XXX) the city is discovered, but first an intermediating vision of transfigured nature must be worked through. Dante sees a river of light, spray from which becomes rubies falling into golden flowers by the river bank (*Paradiso*, XXX, 55–69). But these are mere shadows ("umbriferi prefazii") due to his defective sight (*Paradiso*, XXX, 80–81). The "Rome" of heaven is then revealed as an architectural phenomenon, an amphitheater, that is simultaneously a rose; and the jeweled landscape, the *locus amoenus*, vanishes.

Dante's New Jerusalem is of the first importance. It is a rethinking of the design of the heavenly city from a structure enclosing a garden to a structure that is simultaneous and continuous with the transfigured nature it envelops and glorifies. It is here, and in the Jerusalem of *Pearl*, that we must realize the inadequacy of a conception so widespread that I shall document it only by one instance, a conception that the city of New Jerusalem is merely an "accepted alternative" to the Garden of Eden as the model for the Paradise to come and that garden and city are "interchangeable 'figures.'"[66] Such an assumption obscures and undermines the hierarchical relationships of *Pearl*, where the dreamer, admitted to the paradisal landscape, is allowed only to see, but not to enter, the city; driven back in his attempt to force an entrance, he awakens.[67] Such a conception ignores not only the appropriateness of an architectural environment for a community but also the revision of Eden's typological role in its final state of assimilation to and within an urban framework. It is in this latter synthesis that Dante's ultimate city is a striking formal triumph.

The translation of Jerusalem to the heaven of the Apocalypse completes the divorce initiated by Ezekiel between site and sanctity. When the original and authoritative city lies above, sacred space or sacred precincts on earth may be claimed for any spot that reproduces the divine model. "Paradise" on earth is thus a kind of waiting room, an anticipatory suburb of kingdom come, as the etymology of *parvis*, the place of assembly before a church, suggests; "paradise" also signifies an area of the nave. In both instances "paradise" in its earthly mode is assimilated to sacred spaces that offer access to the celestial city within an architectural framework.

The survival of Eden is a more complicated matter, made so, on the one hand, by the early and enormously popular conflation of the Genesis garden with classical motifs of the golden age, and, on the other, by the conception of a postlapsarian Eden surviving but inaccessible either because it is atop a mountain or because it is remote and fortified. Christian-Latin poets and their successors were authorized by Justin Martyr and St. Augustine to describe Eden in language and figures of speech borrowed from Greek and Latin poetry;[68] it was a commonplace that the golden age was an imperfect recollection of Eden (see, for example, *Purgatorio*, XXVIII, 139–44). But it is not in the elaboration of glosses on Genesis but in the figurative re-creation of Eden in both sacred and profane literature that the garden acquires its new lease on life. It does so in two ways, or in two guises, that may or may not exist together: as the *hortus deliciarum* or "garden of delights," and as the *hortus conclusus* or "walled garden."

In the seventh century Isidore of Seville defined Eden at once as *hortus deliciarum*,[69] and the shift in our conception of Eden from the garden of the drama of Genesis to a Paradise of pleasures that we can imagine enjoying ourselves lies at the root of centuries of literary *loci amoeni*, delightful spots the seriousness of whose Edenic "content" varies a great deal. Classical Elysia and Celtic and other sources furnished also a stock of motifs and sets for visionary and romance literature,[70] in which the Edenic component might be profound or merely decorative. Some sense of the devaluation of the term and notion of *paradise* and the risks in attributing transcendence to the gardens of medieval and Renaissance literature may be gained from Lorenzo de' Medici's genial observation that

"paradise" . . . means nothing more than a most pleasant garden, abundant with all pleasing and delightful things, of trees, apples, flowers, vivid running waters, song of birds and in effect, all the amenities dreamed of by the heart of man; and by this one can affirm that paradise was where there was a beautiful woman, for here was a copy of every amenity and sweetness that a kind heart might desire.[71]

Understood as a Paradise of pleasure, the Edenic *locus amoenus* achieved its definitive iconography in A.D. 398 in Claudian's *Epithalamium* on the marriage of Emperor Honorius Augustus. Claudian describes Venus's jeweled garden atop a mountain but situates a jeweled palace in the middle of it.[72] This conflation of hortulan and architectural models of Paradise (it is a divine residence) passed variously into secular and sacred, homiletic and adventurous, pious and profane verse; it is the source of descriptions of "paradise" that in their repetition of a few motifs, such as garden, pavilion, and fountain, provide a backdrop for religious or erotic allegory and quickly establish the place as both exquisite and hard to get to. We satisfy an appetite not for the transcendent but for the fabulous: for example, in Robert Grosseteste's thirteenth-century *Chasteau d'Amour*, a castle from which four streams issue, conflating the rivers of Eden with the holy city, represents the Virgin's body.

These are "otherworldly" settings of the kind Howard Rollin

Patch has brought together; they borrow Paradise at less than the full theological rate and even in the case of sacred allegory constitute a landscape of romance. And as a matter of romance, paradisal motifs cease to influence our search for the real thing. The "paradises" reported by fabulous travelers like Marco Polo, associated with legendary figures like the emperor Prester John, or recorded in romances like the thirteenth-century *Huon de Bordeaux* are secular structures that anticipate the playgrounds of medieval and Renaissance aristocratic fantasy. Paradise might "survive" in literary and artistic representations of the Fortunate Isles, the land of the Hyperboreans, or the land of Cockaigne; principally it survived as a literary figure of that which is most desirable and most difficult to obtain. In the Renaissance the Edenic garden loses even its claim to being a voyager's ultimate destination. The otherworldly gardens of Ariosto, Spenser, and Tasso are the culminating paradise-gardens of secular literature: metaphors of states of mind, moral gardens and structures rather than transcendent ones, through which heroes pass en route to their real destiny.

The walled garden serves many of the same literary functions as the Claudian version, but it is a figure of greater suggestiveness, having Canticles in the immediate background. The walling of Eden is a condition of its survival in the postlapsarian world, where, strictly speaking, it should have no function except to entertain Enoch and Elijah. But thereby it becomes a matter of romantic quest, a "Matter of Eden" that appears, for example, in the Alexander legends.[73] The power of the walled garden as a figure seems to depend more on its walls than on the garden within them. If Paradise is the place of fulfillment and enclosed places are the most fulfilled, then the phenomenology of the walled garden is explicitly paradisal, no matter if the kind of fulfillment happens to be spiritual or merely erotic. Both the Claudian and the walled Edenic models are images of the inaccessible and the desirable, but whereas the former is truly remote, the latter may be tantalizingly close.

16

In Lucas Cranach's *The Golden Age*, ca.
1530, the walls, trees and fountain of the
conventional paradisal icon frame an
aristocratic erotic fantasy. In the
background are the cities and castles of
real, nonparadisal life.

17

The Garden of Love in the *Roman de la
Rose*, from a late fifteenth-century
manuscript, the most widely diffused
translation of the paradisal garden of
Genesis/Canticles into secular literature.

Diffused throughout medieval literature, the two models maintain a constant mythical and moral pressure upon the variously pious and profane works that they adorn; but the price paid is the integrity of the original Eden. Where every foursquare garden is Edenic, every landscape of palace and garden paradisal, none can be very much so. It is perhaps in reaction as much to the persistent seriousness of the Edenic figure as to its frivolous use that Milton disposes of Eden once and for all. In *Paradise Lost*, Michael describes to Adam how the flood will strip the entire mount of Paradise and push it

> Down the great River to the op'ning Gulf,
> And there take root an Iland salt and bare,
> The haunt of Seals and Orcs, and Sea-mews clang.
> To teach thee that God attributes to place
> No sanctitie, if none be thither brought
> By Men who there frequent, or therein dwell.
> (XI, 833–38)

There is another kind of Edenic survival, in literature formally termed *pastoral* and *georgic* and in the large body of imaginative fiction and nonfiction that restates and continues pastoral and georgic values. Because pastoral (loosely, literature celebrating rural or natural ease) and georgic (literature celebrating agricultural life) withdraw outward to the countryside or backward to the past, they customarily contradict the values of epic and adventurous literature and in a large sense may be seen as rejections of the "future." Both kinds of literature consistently locate vice and degeneracy in the city and in values associated with urban life, and some of the tensions between these New Edens and the varieties of New Jerusalems will be examined in subsequent chapters.

The subversion of Jerusalem is, however, difficult where the conviction is fixed that the past was of its nature different or that nature, human and otherwise, has changed. That the secular impulse to utopia is rooted in a predisposition to favor the use of art over nature or the use of art to transform or regenerate nature is suggested by a summary of the modern utopian credo: it is a partitioning of nature—human and otherwise—into two parts:

There is to be contrivance where there once was an easy and untaught spontaneity; there is to be knowledge where there once was ignorance; there is to be morality where there once was innocence; there is to be community where there once was anarchy; there is to be civilization where once was rawness. There is to be harmony in modern utopia, as there was harmony in the old natural conditions; but harmony on a higher level. Perfection now presupposes complication.[74]

The special significance of the New Jerusalem of the Apocalypse lies both in its assimilation and subordination of the Yahwist garden and in its triumphant deployment of the metal that is a primary topos of the iron age. Hidden in the bowels of the earth, gold never corrupted the men of the age ironically styled golden, but as the principal tool of fallen civilization, gold is the equivalent of architecture: both are metonymic for craft, as Seneca argues in his *Moral Epistle* 90. The shift from Eden to Jerusalem requires the assimilation of the forbidden treasure to the structure of Paradise; here, where no corruption is possible, the incorruptible substance is apotheosized, manifesting not only the preciousness of the New Jerusalem, as Bunyan observes, but the great pains taken to erect the city (since gold is difficult to find, to transport, and so on).[75]

Bunyan's reading is merely symbolic, but no symbolism obstructs our understanding of the compensation afforded by this abundance— the inverse of a prohibition. In a like way the city compensates us for Sodom and Babylon.[76] Now the negative formulas of the golden age are turned back upon their formulators—the praisers of passed time— and the root of all evils, or its principal symbol, is flaunted. The lapsarian craft of (gold) mining, assimilated to the nobler but still lapsarian craft of building, points up, as a reconstituted garden could not, the transformation of the *civitas terrena* ("earthly city") into the city where our highest inventive (not "natural") capacities are shaped to vivifying rather than to morbid ends. The vision is antiarcadian both topically and ontologically: topically in that the Paradise of nature and rest, both Yahwist and classical, is crushed beneath that of artifice and celebration; ontologically in that man's real nature is seen to fulfill itself in the latter rather than in the former conditions. The will to transform the stuff of commercial riches into the emblem of eternal bliss informs such a vision of a city of gold as that of the French architect Michel Ragon, who speculates upon a new city unified as a single building,[77] freed by new structural mechanisms from the law of gravity:

C'est la technique legère des *ossatures actuelles* qui fait virer l'expression architectonique en y incorporant *le silence et la transparence du ciel.*[78]

TWO

Poet and Architect

Believe me, that was a happy age, before architects,
before builders!

(SENECA, *Moral Epistle* 90)

If, then, the universe is the effect of some act; that act itself,
the effect of a Being, and of a need, a thought, a knowledge,
and a power which belongs to that Being, it is then only by
an act that you can rejoin the grand design, and undertake
the imitation of that which has made all things. And that
is to put oneself in the most natural way in the very place
of the God.

Now, of all acts the most complete is that of
constructing.

(PAUL VALÉRY, *Eupalinos, or, The Architect*)

The disparity between the architectural achievements of classical
civilization and architecture's place in antique aesthetic and philo-
sophical systems is a curious instance of the relative absence of a
body of Greek and Roman opinion on what are now called "the fine
arts." Because classical philosophers before Plotinus distinguish
among the arts according to criteria unrelated to aesthetics in the
modern senses of the word (the study of the beautiful and the
sublime, for example), no clear exposition of the nature and importance of architecture is formulated or, if formulated, finds wide
acceptance.[1] Because it produces real things rather than images of
things, "building" has merit in Plato's eyes (*Sophist* 219A, 235C–
236C, 265B; *Republic* 601D), and as an art that completes nature
it ought to please Aristotle (*Physics* 199a15). But because it fails to

47

imitate, it cannot be a fine art, for its primitive type or model is not found in the exterior world,[2] and so Aristotle leaves it where medieval philosophers would, with greater refinement, also locate it: as a mechanical art, for instance, as a subdivision of fortification, as Hugh of St. Victor so classifies it in the twelfth century.[3]

There is some theoretical reinforcement: Vitruvius, though alone among architectural theorists, survived antiquity, and St. Augustine linked architecture with music in a formula that was to have great consequences for medieval builders.[4] In his Socratic dialogue *Eupalinos, ou, l'architecte* Paul Valéry has pursued the implications of this respectful equation, developing the argument that "act" is superior to "thought." But for the moment—the moment of the Graeco-Roman millennium, roughly from the time of Hesiod to that of Constantine—Socrates's praise of Aristides at the expense of Themistocles (*Gorgias* 455, 503, 526) better points up the linking of "architecture" to a pattern of rhetorical tropes keyed to normative conceptions of desirable and undesirable behavior: Aristides filled Athens with virtue, Themistocles with public works. This is a trope of dystopia, architectural projects synecdochically standing for the (over-) built city, to which wealth and effort is misdirected, and it is a quarry that poet and philosopher pursue with relish. As emblem of the condition of fallen or degenerated human nature, architecture is evidence that compatibility with nature—the natural world, and human nature properly understood—has been lost.

That primal compatibility of man and nature is understood as either "hard" or "soft,"[5] finding expression in the arcadian literature of a golden age where no labor was required or in the georgic literature of one where honest toil was readily rewarded. The advantage of the latter is that it can be recaptured not only in poetry but in real life on the farm. The poetic texts in which the various terms of the myth were set forth are well known, and have been extensively examined;[6] from Hesiod's *Works and Days* and Aratus's *Phaenomena* the tale descended to Ovid, who codified the four metallic ages (gold, silver, bronze, and iron) that identify the progressive degeneration of man and society (*Metamorphoses* I, 89–150); and it descended to Virgil and to Horace, celebrators of country life. Houses, like agriculture, find their place within the myth as creations of the degenerate silver age, and the final age of iron embraces typical occupations of the Roman world like seafaring and mining and is distinguished by warfare, injustice, infidelity, and impiety. In the celebration of rural living Virgil and Horace invoke the irrecoverable golden world, whose tutelary deity Astraea (Δίκη, or Justice) last dwelled among farmers.[7]

The pattern of progressive degeneration, then, is interrupted and complicated by the existence of the neogolden rural society adjacent to the ferric and feral one of Rome and the city. In the contemporary countryside the practice of crafts, which is generally an iron age activity, is tolerated or approved to the extent that such activities fulfill only the minimal necessities of well-regulated lives and are seen as harmoniously related to those lives. So the iron age of the modern city stands in contrast not only to a pastoral golden world of unhoused shepherds and nomads nourished by a paradisal soil but also to the georgic farming community of modestly sheltered toilers, whom the kindly earth meets as though halfway.

Central to the force of this latter opposition are architectural tropes of the kind Plato used against Themistocles; most representative are the *aurea laquearia*, the "golden ceilings" (coffered or paneled and gilded).[8] Their reputed viciousness is a chapter in the history of the war on luxury, begun by Plato in Book II of the *Republic* and continuing through a literature too vast to be examined here except in its specifically architectural instances.[9] In a career, however, beginning at least in Dido's banqueting hall in the *Aeneid* (I, 726) and continuing at least to Pandaemonium in *Paradise Lost* (I, 717), "the roof was fretted gold" is a touchstone of vice, a classic instance of the moral tradition of literary architecture. "Vice infects the very wall," Andrew Marvell wrote of a convent,[10] and the vicious houses and palaces of classical moralists infect the society within and without. Ritually denounced by Virgil, Horace, Martial, Juvenal, and Pliny, and despite the wrath of Isidore, St. Cyprian, St. Ambrose, and St. Jerome, *aurea laquearia* survive as the staple of depraved interior decoration. In the seventeenth century, Richard Crashaw is quick to assure us that we shall find "no roofs of gold o'er riotous tables shining"—in a nunnery.[11]

A stern tone is adopted toward the indulgences of a younger world. Eustathius's twelfth-century commentary on Homer served as model and precedent for Alexander Pope's contemptuous characterization of Alcinous's splendid and idyllic estate (*Odyssey* VII): a "pompous" house, Pope remarks in a note to his translation of Homer, "excellently agrees with the vain *Alcinous*."[12] Horace's *Epode* 2 offers a well-known example of the "doorsill trope" in literary architecture: *Beatus ille qui procul negotiis / Ut prisca gens mortalium,* "happy the man who far from business affairs, like the first race of men" avoids "the haughty thresholds of too-powerful citizens," *superba civium / potentiorum limina.* These components of domestic construction are engaged with their owners in an active exchange of bad habits, and are ultimately anthropomorphic, participating in the behavior of those dwelling within while exerting a moral pressure so pervasive that it remains a touchstone of modernist architectural rhetoric. In a chapter revealingly called "Integrity: In a House as in an Individual," Frank Lloyd Wright affirms that "an irresponsible, flashy, pretentious or dishonest individual would never be happy in such a house as we now call organic because of this quality of integrity."[13]

Organic is, of course, a rich word; rhetorical tropes of the splendid, evil structure or of its ceiling, lintel, or whatever intend to recall to us the time when man, in the absence of crafts for which architecture metonymically stands, lived with his own kind as well as within nature in the sort of relationship suggested by *organic,* and these tropes direct us also to admire the life of the countryside where structures exist in a "natural" balance with legitimate human needs. In his *Moral Epistle* 90, a general assault on all artisanship, Seneca codifies the literary arguments into a powerful diatribe. Proceeding from the axiom that man loses his mastery over the whole world when he seeks to appropriate some part of it to himself (*Desierunt enim omnia possidere, dum volunt propria*), Seneca distinguishes the iron age of marble and brick from that "happy age, before the days of architects, before the days of builders!"[14] And he supplies the cause, mysteriously absent in Hesiod and Ovid, of the skid from those golden years: man fell when desire was born. Passing rapidly from the first illegitimate urge for artificial shelter to the Golden House in Rome (and its gilded ceilings; see p. 75 below), he concludes, perhaps appropriately in the case of Nero's enormous villa, *nunc magna pars nostri metus tecta sunt* ("today our houses make up a great part of our dread").

Seneca's explanation of the Fall from Paradise is psychological, but the consequences of that Fall are ethical and show up in man's behavior to man: "Eyes that cannot tolerate marble unless it is mottled and polished with recent rubbing, that at home would rather see under foot only pavements more costly than gold," may cheerfully ignore filth and misery outdoors.[15] The argument anticipates that of medieval economics, grounded on assumptions about the appropriation of wealth and the misdirection of labor; twelve centuries later, a French bishop, Hugue de Fouilloi, will denounce the "wonderful but perverted delectation" of luxurious episcopal apartments as, in effect, a withholding of charity from the poor.[16] He echoes, among others, such early Christian authorities as Tatian, St. Clement, Origen, and St. John Chrysostom. The extreme but unimpeachable response to architecture, and to all the world as understood through the five senses, is that of St. Bernard of Clairvaux (1090–1153), who so mortified his faculties that upon emerging from a year's solitary confinement, he was unable to recall that his chamber was vaulted or that it had three windows rather than one.[17] The primary juncture between classical and Christian hostility to the material is found in the assimilation in patristic thought of the portrait of the passionless philosopher to that of Adam, who, it was generally agreed, "had no house, ate fruit and vegetables, prayed, labored, and experienced no sexual passion."[18] If the simplest definition of luxury is "*anything unneeded*,"[19] then the wall that encloses the paradisal gardens of literature is from the stoic perspective a luxury and an accretion upon Adam's pristine and hortulan state.

Yet there is plenty of evidence of a divided state of mind. On one occasion, Cicero inveighs against the profligate Chrysogonos by taxing his splendid mansion with responsibility for the corruption it shelters, yet elsewhere he ranks architecture with education and medicine, and in a pleasant letter he advises his brother on the decoration of an elaborate villa.[20] Like Statius and Pliny, who write eloquently of the material beauties of country estates,[21] Cicero can construct a portrait of well-heeled suburban life without reference to the moral tradition governing the conventional critiques. In a famous epigram, Martial insists upon the fructifying influence of a simple homestead and the sterilizing pall cast over the landscape by a fancy piece of architectural goods, but elsewhere he enthusiastically recommends Domitian's new palace in Rome.[22] Doubtless in the latter instance he merely showed himself prudent, but his praise is significant because its cosmic terminology refers as strongly as do stoic condemnations of craft to a powerful literary and social myth. In Martial's poem a god-king is seen to dwell in a celestial space, which has been set upon the Palatine Hill by the architect's ingenuity. *Astra polumque pia cepisti mente*, he says to him—"you have caught heaven and the firmament in your worthy intellect."

We are likely to understand Martial's praise metaphorically, but Domitian probably took it at face value. As a claim for the palace as well as for the emperor, the verses contribute to a literary tradition that articulates the silent rhetoric of paradisal architecture, and that constitutes a point of view contrary to the conventional literary position. The architectural rhetoric itself is of two related kinds: "sacred" and "utopian" are approximate terms that indicate the shift from sacred or literally paradisal structures to those on a more human scale, not transcendent but in some sense virtuous.

Buildings that fall into both categories share common roots in the status conferred upon them by the physical properties of their materials, and it is to the literary treatment of numinous or ideal architecture that we must first turn. Subsequently, we must examine three phenomena that may occur singly or in combination in architecture: ideal proportions, an ideal grammar of surfaces or ornamentation, and ideal forms or architectural components. All three in various ways have been conceived as not only representative of the celestial city or state of being but capable of reconstituting it.

In the case both of proportions, or spatial relationships, and of fidelity to a prototypically ideal or "correct" articulation of surfaces and ornament, one building serves as an index to the paradisal or ecstatic component in architecture:

as it is the Basis of all that may be seen Magnificent in Architecture, now a-dayes, it may serve as a Patern throughout the whole, by which all the Branches belonging to Architecture must be proved and ordered.[23]

The Temple of Solomon possessed unique authority over the architectural as well as the theological mind of the Jewish and Christian worlds at least until the late eighteenth century, and it was repeatedly "copied" according to the variously conceived reconstitutions of its physical proportions and its design. In classical architecture, by contrast, there was no equivalent building; there sanctity was thought to be transmitted through the reproduction, often in a loose or allusive manner, of constituents of sacred structures, such as the dome. At various moments in architectural history in the Mediterranean and European worlds, single buildings, collections of buildings, and entire cities acquire or, at least, lay claim to the paradisal and numinous properties deriving from these different sources, both elementary and sophisticated.

IDEAL AND EPIC ARCHITECTURE

An architecture of Paradise can be recognized at the point when certain phenomena of actual or imagined earthly structures are understood to have the effect of etherealizing those structures. Abstracted from those structures, these rarefied or immortal constituents furnish the vocabulary of a celestial architecture, which itself comes to be seen as the model for terrestrial antitypes. Transferred from the antitypes themselves, normally temple and palace, these phenomena pass into secular architecture, conferring upon it associations with the supernatural or numinous. The process is one of the intellectualization both of sensory perceptions and of the pleasure felt in those perceptions; virtue in both senses of the word—excellence and potency—is perceived as inhering in specific formal properties of space and matter. These properties—or phenomena or constituents of forms—may be variously classified, but in the main they are ideality of shape, hardness of surface, brilliance of surface, great mass, multiplication of units, and ideality or complexity of plan. These are the tools of the architect.

An appreciation of the special significance of the square, the circle, the cube, and the sphere is, for example, central to an appreciation of sacred architecture, whether or not these and other geometric forms are, in a Jungian sense, archetypes.[24] The square as symbol of the moral perfection of man and the unity of the Church had manifested itself in the replicated squares and cubes of Solomon's Temple, which is distinguished in Scripture, like Noah's ark and the tabernacle before it, by precise accounting and repetition of proportions. The English poet George Wither's 1635 emblem, a clear visual reference to Revelation 21, is glossed as a symbol of the perfect man

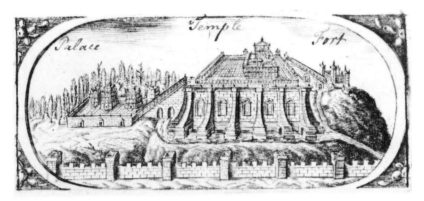

18

It was difficult to think of the Temple as a
succession of different structures, and,
typically, Solomon's, Ezekiel's, and Herod's
were conflated, as in Jacob Judah Leon's
popular and anachronistic drawing of
Solomon's Temple and palace and the
Herodian fortress, the Antonia, 1642, in
*An Accurate Description of the Grand and
Glorious Temple of Solomon*, tr. M. P.
DeCastro, London, 1778.

19

The figure of the perfect man, engraving
from George Wither's *A Collection of
Emblemes*, 1635.

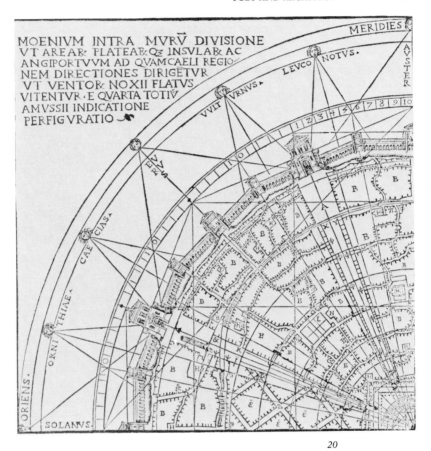

20

After Vitruvius, *De Architectura* I, 6, the
plan of an ideal city laid out to accord with
the prevailing winds, from Cesare di
Lorenzo Cesariano's edition, Como, Italy,
1521 (facsimile edition, Bronx, N.Y.:
Blom, 1968).

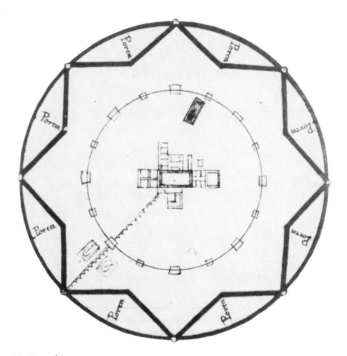

21, 22, and 23

Ideal cities of the Italian Renaissance:
Filarete's plan for Sforzinda, from his
Trattato d'Architettura, 1470 (facsimile
edition, New Haven: Yale University
Press, 1965); after Buonaiuto Lorini, from
his *Delle Fortificatione Libri Cinque*, 1592;
and after Vincenzo Scamozzi, from his
L'Idea della Architettura Universale, 1615.

24

An ideal city, Francesco di Giorgio,
Perspective of a Square, ca. 1470.

who will become a building block of the spiritual temple; the identical appearance presented by the cube, "wherever borne," figures the constant soul, however tossed, and, anagogically, the smallest unit of the spiritual stones that make up the community of the blessed.

Herodotus describes Ecbatana as girdled with concentric, ascending walls (*Histories* I, 98); like many other ancient or lost cities, such as the Baghdad of the caliphate, it integrated simple cosmological symbolism into its plan and system of fortifications. Such symbolism is utopian as well as cosmological in Plato's imaginary cities, those of the *Laws*, where the town is circular, and of the *Timaeus* and the *Critias*, where, in the layout of Atlantis, square and circle are juxtaposed. St. Augustine understood the circle as a symbol of virtue and anagogically representative of virtue "because of the conformity and concordance of its essentials";[25] Rudolf Arnheim has examined the symbolic importance of circular structures and plans as against the square; the circle is self-contained whereas the square implies other squares.[26] Ideal planning in consonance with a pure geometric form dictates the plan of Vitruvius's ideal city, patterned to take advantage of the winds. Whatever mystique may inhere in the circle is here projected upon the plane of pragmatic urban design and furnishes the prototype for Renaissance experiments of a generally military nature, like Filarete's Sforzinda of 1470, and for ideal plans like those of Buonaiuto Lorini and Vincenzo Scamozzi in the following two centuries. In these instances a high degree of abstraction calls attention to geometrical values as ends in themselves and as the special project of the architect and the planner. Yet the purely mystical dimension may survive in the typical placement of a *tempietto* or other circular structure in the center of a town designed along the principle of the square, as in Francesco di Giorgio's cityscape of about 1470; the man-centered, ideal city reserves the place of honor for the circular structure evoking a higher order.[27]

Behind the deployment of ideal geometries lies a more immediate and sensuous identification of excellence with the phenomena of mass and luminosity. These are present at the inception of Western literature in the palaces of Alcinous and Menelaus in the *Odyssey*. Though briefly described, Menelaus's walls are shining (παμφἀνόωντα); the hall is lofty (ὑψερεφέs). Telemachus and his companions, strangers from a rougher province, show their awe at the precious metals and gems, the ivory, the sheen of the baths; the brilliance is compared to that of the sun and the moon, with which the palace is symbolically aligned (*Odyssey* IV). At the palace of Alcinous, Odysseus himself, in Robert Fitzgerald's translation,

> meditated a long time before crossing
> the brazen threshold of the great courtyard.
> High rooms he saw ahead, airy and luminous
> as though with lusters of the sun and moon,
> bronze-panelled walls, at several distances,
> making a vista, with an azure molding
> of lapis lazuli. The doors were golden
> guardians of the great room. Shining bronze
> plated the wide door sill; the post and lintel
> were silver upon silver; golden handles
> curved on the doors. . . .[28]

"These were the gifts of Heaven to Alkinoos [sic]" (*Odyssey* VII, 132). This royal enclosure (buildings within courtyards) corresponds to Zeus's palace, which also boasts a bronze doorsill (*Iliad* I, 426) and to that of Hephaestus (*Iliad* XVIII, 368ff.): "well-built" (ἐὔσταθέοs), "glittering" (ἀστερόεντα), and wholly bronze, a rather impracticable building material even in the bronze age.[29] Ovid's *Regia Solis* (*Metamorphoses* II), a literary building that stands behind all late Latin and medieval paradise-castles (it is the prototype for Claudian's in his *Epithalamium* on Emperor Honorius Augustus), is a full-dress presentation of the theme:

sublimibus alta columnis
clara micante auro flammasque imitante pyropo,
cuius ebur nitidum fastigia summa tegebat,
argenti bifores radiabant lumine valvae.

This "Palace of the Sun" stood

high on lofty columns, bright with glittering gold and bronze that
shone like fire. Gleaming ivory crowned the gables above; the double
folding doors were radiant with burnished silver.[30]

Aldous Huxley has observed, in *Heaven and Hell*, that these hard,
glittering materials are one of the few characteristics of Paradise upon
which we may rely because testimony from those who say they have
been there is so consistent on this point. Their terrestrial antitypes
integrate as much gold or bronze into their architecture as the poet
thinks credible while adding allusions to celestial motions that
deepen the correspondence.

Menelaus hesitated, however, to allow the analogy to be made,
warning Telemachus not to presume a familiarity with the courts of
Zeus (*Odyssey* IV, 71ff.); but the *Beowulf* poet is prepared to drive the
connection home. Heorot, Hrothgar's royal seat, is a wine-hall that
boasts a gift-throne, where the valiant enjoy rest, feast, and their lord's
love.[31] Its construction, Alvin Lee has argued, is mimetic of the
Creation, which is in fact the subject of the scop's first song in the
newly built hall. Heorot is the antithesis of the terrifying landscape
that shelters the Grendels, a landscape that, however, *in illo tempore*,
God fashioned with love:

> wlitebeorhtne wang   swā waeter bebugeð,
> gesette sigehrēþig   sunnan ond mōnan
> lēoman tō lēohte   landbūendum
> ond gefraetwade   foldan scēatas
> leomum und lēafum. . . .

> fair-bright field   which water surrounds,
> set up triumphant   sun and moon
> gleaming as light   for land-dwellers
> and adorned   earth's regions
> with limbs and leaves. . . .[32]

The *wlitebeorhtne wang* is lost; its luminous and verdant qualities survive in the gilding and in the woven wall hangings of Heorot (lines 991–96). Here is a provisional security in a fallen world, the wall Eden lacked. Middle term in a sequence of paradises, Heorot recapitulates the landscape of the first age, created "fair-bright" for men while anticipating the communality of the celestial wine-hall where God sits on his gift-throne. Heorot is further linked with celestial mansions by its architectural flourish; the horn-gable (*horngeap*, line 82) occurs elsewhere in Anglo-Saxon poetry only once (in *Andreas*, lines 667–68), in a description of the Temple of Jerusalem.

The fact that Homer devotes more verse to describing Eumaeus's steading than to Priam's palace suggests, however, the unimportance of epic architecture to the characters within most epic poems, whatever the metaphorical and anagogical resonances for an audience. Epic architects are few in name; an exception is Mulciber, the architect of Pandaemonium in *Paradise Lost*, who is Hephaestus or Vulcan, builder of the bronze palace already referred to and of palaces for all the other gods (*Iliad* I, 590ff.). His words are affirmed as meaningful *within* the dramatic narrative of *Paradise Lost*. Both the act of construction and the design of Pandaemonium serve as a comment not only upon Satan's pretensions to transcendence but also upon the ambiguous moral status of the artisan, who in Seneca's complaint asks how rather than why an act should be performed.

To build Pandaemonium, the fallen angels "Op'nd into the Hill a spacious wound / And dig'd out ribs of Gold" (I, 689–90). Having thereby violated an antique taboo on mining, they construct

a Temple, where *Pilasters* round
Were set, and Doric pillars overlaid
With Golden Architrave; nor did there want
Cornice or Freeze, with bossy Sculptures grav'n,
The Roof was fretted Gold.
                    (I, 713–17)

Artificial lights "as from a sky" hang from this fretted, "arched roof" (I, 726), that is, domed or barrel-vaulted classical ceiling; "roof" signifies "ceiling" here, as in *laquearia*, which has both senses.[33]

Hell is not, however, to be condemned as urban as against a purely pastoral landscape of heaven;[34] heaven is elaborately walled, and Pandaemonium lies more or less in the center of an unmeasurable expanse of "Rocks, Caves, Lakes, Fens, Bogs, Dens" (II, 621). The iconographical background to hell is that of the paradisal pavilion in the paradisal landscape; and the constituents of sacred architecture, including density, tight focus, and progressive and intensive organization of mass and space, are here deployed in an ironical rejection of "Jerusalem" and of the Claudian paradisal mode. We perceive Pandaemonium in a hostile landscape as a place of refuge, the one locus of organization, but it exacts its price; claustrophobia arises not only from the famous shrinkage of the angels to fit inside (I, 777ff.) but also from the relentless glitter of metals and chemicals ("*Naphtha* and *Asphaltus*"). Pandaemonium is experienced not as a city but as a room—as the pavilion that it is; it is a dystopia of the indoors. That it is an exact inversion of the order of celestial space in *Paradise Lost* serves as a comment upon all earthly "temples" organized in like fashion, discounted by the Holy Ghost (I, 17–18) in favor of "th'upright heart and pure."

Milton's disapproval of an earthly temple is, however, a late and subtle position, hardly to be reconciled with Jehovah's commission to the Hebrews (Exodus 25:8) for precious metals, gems, and expensive stuffs to furnish "a sanctuary, that I may dwell among them." In his

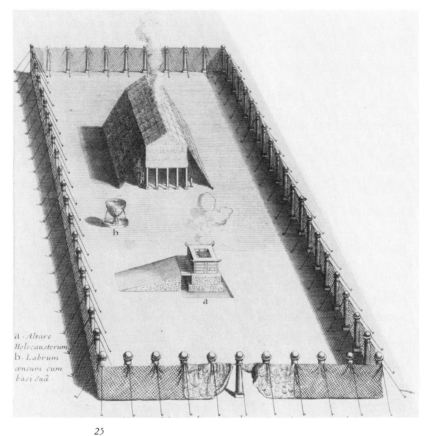

25

The tabernacle in the desert, prototype for
the Temple, as reconstructed by Bernard
Lamy, from his *De Tabernaculo Foederis, De
Sancta Civitate Jerusalem, et de Templo eius
Libri Septem*, Paris, 1720.

26

Modern reconstruction of the Temple of
Solomon by Theodore Busink, from his
*Der Tempel von Jerusalem von Salamo bis
Herodes*, Leiden: Brill, 1970.

longest direct address to the human race, God descends to details of curtain rods and fabric selection, thus implicitly legitimizing both architecture and its attendant crafts, as well as authorizing the use of splendid materials. In the succeeding Temple of Solomon, splendor of surfaces and decorations is united to the ideal, replicated geometric spaces (1 Kings 6:2-3) that complete the localization of celestial space on earth. The significance of the Temple cannot be separated from its appearance. Ruskin singles out its richness as, paradoxically, an expression of humility rather than of pride; it is an example of the quality he calls "sacrifice," the signification of the unstinting nature of worship. God requires tribute

not only of the fruits of the earth and the tithe of time, but of all treasures of wisdom and beauty; of the thought that invents, and the hand that labours; of wealth of wood, and weight of stone; of the strength of iron, and the light of gold.[35]

What did it look like? "There is hardly a harder task in Study," wrote John Lightfoot in 1650, "than to describe structures and places not seen, and at a distance, and the Scripture hath hardly a more obscure description of anything than this fabricke."[36] The scriptural obscurity lies not only in the absence of data from which to derive a section or elevation of the Temple but in the ambiguous relationship of the various parts of the plan as it can be inferred from the recorded dimensions. The account given in 2 Chronicles (probably of the fourth century B.C.) enlarges the dimensions of 1 Kings (ca. 550 B.C.);[37] Ezekiel's visionary reconstruction (also of the sixth century B.C.; Ezekiel 40–48) is very different from the Solomonic structure;[38] Zerubbabel's reconstruction of ca. 500 B.C. was apparently strikingly inferior (see above, p. 27); and Herod's of the late first century B.C. was strikingly Hellenistic.[39] Viewed synoptically as it has nearly always been, as a single Solomonic Temple correctly reconstructed (or envisioned) on each occasion, the Temple would at the very least have to be the size of the largest version, that of Ezekiel.

To Christian architects, however, reconstituting the Temple has rarely meant rebuilding it, any more than in the Christian city they have tried to mimic destroyed Jerusalem. The architectural significance of the Temple lay, for medieval and Renaissance architects, primarily in the immaterial proportions conferring special status upon it because they came from God. This conception of an abstract system of proportions constituting a divine model is one of the strongest and most continuous links between Gothic and Renaissance architects, both adhering to the Pythagorean concept that "All is Number."[40] As Otto von Simson has argued, the restored Temple of Ezekiel's vision was understood in medieval thought to prefigure the heavenly city but not in subjection to any particular style or system of construction and ornament. What to the patron and architect of the Gothic cathedral distinguished their efforts was submission to geometry as a system of perfect relationships.[41] That architecture mirrors divine forms mathematically is implicit in Augustinian aesthetics, which anchor true beauty in metaphysical reality, finding it chiefly in the arts governed by the immutable numerical ratios of Pythagorean mysticism: music and architecture.[42] As restated by Peter Abelard in the twelfth century, the analogy between the two arts obviated any obligation to be faithful to surfaces, which in the case of the Temple would have been impossible, or to a specific plan; rather, it was essential to follow the ideal consonances of the Temple in shaping the interior spaces of the cathedral.

Thus, the dimensions given in 1 Kings 6:2 of sixty, twenty, and thirty cubits for the length, width, and height—as well as the ratio between cella, aula, and porch, and the cubic dimensions of the Holy of Holies—correspond to Platonic perfect consonances.[43] The system of correspondence was elaborately worked out at the Cathedral School of Chartres[44] and amplifies not only St. Augustine's analogy of music to architecture but also Plato's metaphor of the universe as matter informed by geometry; perfect proportions knit the universe into a whole and are explicitly tectonic as well as technical.[45] The Temple thus corresponds to the cosmos and to the heavenly city, and its proportions govern the cathedral that has the same function:

If the architect designed his sanctuary according to the laws of harmonious proportion, he did not only imitate the order of the visible world, but conveyed an intimation, inasmuch as that is possible to man, of the perfection of the world to come.[46]

In the great luminosity of Gothic architecture particularly, the free reconstitution of the Temple's immaterial dimensions is joined to the metaphorical reconstitution of its glitter—the glitter of the five thousand tons of gold with which Solomon reputedly plated it.[47] In the twelfth century, Abbot Suger of Saint-Denis, taking literally St. Paul's architectural metaphors (Ephesians 2:19ff.), wrote in his *De Consecratione* that the church served to reconcile cosmic discordancies;[48] his translator, the Benedictine scholar Dom Jean Le Clerc, argued that "edification" was not merely a metaphor but should recall to us its root meaning and that sacred architecture, "requiring the vision of divine glory for its design but physical labor for its material construction," was "the perfect realization of the Benedictine concept of labor as a process of edification";[49] and thus architecture assumed an ethical as well as an eschatological function, not only representing Paradise to men but preparing them to enter it.

MORPHOLOGIES OF THE HOLY CITY

The early history of Christian architecture is in large part a description of how imperial architectural forms and components were assimilated or converted to religious use while retaining the prestige that characterized their earlier functions. Thus, the colonnaded forecourts or "atria" before earlier churches were not dictated by liturgical necessity but transferred to the churches the semidivinity that attached to the emperor when, in such a forecourt of a basilica, he conventionally appeared before the people.[50] This is one example among many of paradisal architectural rhetoric, here passing not from the perfect proportions of the Temple to its avatars but from various imperial architectural forms to their more or less faithful duplication in specifically sacred architecture. In the case of Jerusalem, the sanctity of the Temple had long since passed to the city itself, whose Christian structures came to acquire the power of prototypes. The erection of a "copy," however loose, of a sacred structure in Jerusalem such as the Church of the Holy Sepulchre, could be seen as a transfer or acquisition of sacred space both because of the function of the prototype and because of its specific architectural constituents. Or the architectural "content" might be altogether a matter of function: the Roman church of Santa Croce in Gerusalemme, founded by Constantine to receive pieces of the True Cross, was the station for the fourth Sunday in Lent because it was perceived as a "vicarious Jerusalem," a literal representation of Jerusalem in Judaea.[51]

An instance in which the numinous "content" of an architectural element (the dome), and of the city of Jerusalem, and of a specific structure is "moved" and reconstituted has been pointed out by Stephen Nichols, who has shown how Charlemagne sought to shift the prestige of Jerusalem, and of the first and second Rome, to Aachen, in an act that climaxed centuries of architectural mysticism.[52] The circular structures surmounting both the Holy Sepulchre, begun under Constantine, and the tomb of the Virgin, had been imitated at Hagia Soros in Constantinople and in Rome by the convenient dedication of the Pantheon as Sancta Maria ad Martyres in 609 (the further influence of Constantine's Holy Sepulchre has been the subject of modern scholarship).[53] Because the symbolic content rather than the strict design of these structures was what legitimized imitations, or types, we recognize at the climax of the process

Charlemagne's Palatine Chapel, a vaulted octagon surrounded by ambulatory and galleries. By synecdoche, the chapel is the city; Jerusalem has yielded its historical role to Rome and to Constantinople (over all of which Constantine ruled); Constantine was head of state and church; and Charlemagne, crowned emperor in 800, is his successor. Aachen thus qualifies as the *Nova Roma*, as in fact it was named in Carolingian documents, and the emperor was represented in the attitude of Christ or with Christ gesturing to him as regent. "Where the emperor is, there is Rome," according to Herodian (*Histories*, I, vi, 5), and in his capacity as divine autocrat the emperor dwells in his heavenly city as well as on earth. In the case especially of late imperial and subsequent regimes in Europe and the Mediterranean basin, Christian and otherwise, a piece of the celestial city may be said to be localized like an embassy on this planet in structures correspondent to it, as E. Baldwin Smith has argued at length.[54] At the consecration of the church of Saint-Denis in 1144, the king assumed a Christ-like role, and Abbot Suger evidently wished it to be understood that the royal and the celestial dominions were united within the new Gothic enclosure.[55]

The city in its larger aspect may reassume the sacred role or seize it. Perhaps because they misunderstood Urban II's descriptions of Jerusalem as "the navel of the world," "paradise," and "the royal city placed in the center of the world," soldiers of the First Crusade in 1099 apparently expected to find the celestial city at the end of their road.[56] In a sense, they were right. Reestablishment of the kingdom of Jerusalem was seen to restore the proper typological relationship between an earthly and a heavenly city, and a mass specially composed to celebrate the capture of the city presented the conquest as a prefiguration of the attainment of salvation and as actually inducive to that end.[57]

In quattrocento Rome, Nicholas V fused Solomonic typologies with architect Leon Battista Alberti's program for the secular city to body forth the hierarchical structure of Church and state. In the

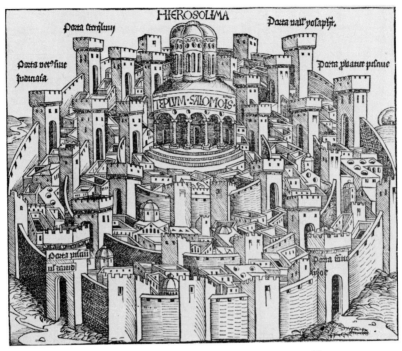

27

The Temple was frequently confused with
the Dome of the Rock, erected on its site
after the Arab conquest of Jerusalem in the
seventh century. "Templum Salomonis"
dominates an idealized circular Jerusalem
in an anonymous 1593 woodcut.

extension to the city, understood architectonically as an arrangement of buildings and spaces, of the numinous content previously inherent in sacred structures, Nicholas V realized Alberti's humanistic intention of education through architecture and his humanistic equation of moral and physical beauty whereas at the Vatican he saw himself, through his extensive construction, as surpassing the Solomon who supposedly imitated his Maker in ordering "all things by measure and number and weight" (Wisdom of Solomon 11:12). In the visible dominance of the ecclesiastic over the new civil architecture, the pope stated through the language of visible forms the authority of the threshold of heaven over the civic community;[58] his was one of many actual or projected programs of the Italian Renaissance, bringing together aristocratic models of the ideal, beautiful city with Judaeo-Christian visions of eternity and authority.[59] And as early as the sixteenth century Philotheus of Pskov, a churchman, declared in a letter to Tsar Vasily III, autocrat and regent of Christ, that Moscow was the third Rome.[60]

The imitation of sacred space perpetuates not only the accidental and historical role of a prototype but the significance of its constituent forms. Not only the immaterial qualities of proportion and luminosity but also specific concrete elements continuously repeat whatever message is thought to inhere in them. The localization of celestial space on earth, regardless of historical or liturgical circumstances, has been elaborately identified by Karl Lehmann with the dome, its ancestors and its analogues, including ceiling, baldachin, and cupola,[61] and E. Baldwin Smith has discovered an extensive celestial symbolism incorporated into the towers of Carolingian abbeys and into the domes of Byzantine churches and palaces, and so at the center of theocratic political programs. An appreciation of the symbolic "content" of these fragments, of specific and entire buildings, and of the "city" considered as an architectural unity, will allow us to grasp the significance of Martial's location of Domitian as the god-king enframed by the domed chamber of his new palace in Rome.

Such an appreciation allows us to understand phenomena not otherwise readily apparent to the eye: how the cluster of eleventh- and
twelfth-century buildings at Santo Stefano, Bologna, was called
"Jerusalem" and was thought to represent the Holy Land, or how
during the Renaissance the *commune* of Brescia prohibited the
destruction of the houses of those condemned for heinous crimes on
the grounds that cities are constructed as models of Paradise.[62]

Such duplications of sacred precincts—as interior spaces or as
arrangements of parts of buildings or of separate buildings—may, as
I have suggested in the instance of the Temple of Solomon, be ex-
tremely subtle, relying altogether on numerical ratios, or they may
be relatively crude approximations, relying on the presumed efficacy of
imitated architectural shapes or arrangements with powerful associations. But sublime proportions need not derive from a sacred text, as
in the case of the Temple, and, by contrast, an imitation may be seen
to re-create and even supplant the Temple by means grosser than
numbers. An understanding of the radically different ways by which a
building attains the status of sacred space can be gained from an
examination of two closely related yet very different "temples," the
Pantheon in Rome and Hagia Sophia in Constantinople.

For it is in these two structures, both culminations of distinct
periods of imperial engineering and design, that we find construction
subordinated to the mystical concept of space that has so dominated
modern architectural thought. "Solids," we are convincingly told,
were for the Romans "of secondary importance to the spaces they
defined; significant hollows, not visible masses, were the essence of
their architecture."[63] The significance of these hollows was largely
worked out in the Golden House, the center of Nero's building
projects at Rome.[64] The grandeur of the Golden House was criticized
by Suetonius, who in Philemon Holland's translation describes sus-
piciously Elizabethan apartments but who takes note of the celestial
pretensions: "But of al these parlours and banqueting roomes, the
principall and fairest was made rounde, to turne about continually

28

The interior of the Pantheon in Rome
defies photography, as the distortions in
the painting by Giovanni Paolo Panini
(ca. 1692–1765) suggest. Both the twisting
postures of the tourists and the illusory
flattening of the walls as they recede
beyond and behind our field of vision
point up the paradox of space that is too
perfect to be grasped accurately by the eye.

both day and night, in manner of the World"–"or," Holland adds in a gloss, "heaven."[65]

In reconstructing Agrippa's Pantheon in Rome, dedicated as the name indicated to all the gods, Hadrian's architects in the next century fully realized the implications of the Neronian dome. William MacDonald has argued that in its design, a dome on a drum, they sought to reduce the gods to equality among themselves, subordinating them to a unitary conception of "Rome" and so literally bringing them down to earth. MacDonald locates the "meaning" of this structure in the superficially awkward transition from the porch to the interior,

> a revelation of an image of the firmament itself. . . . The oculus, the circling coffers, the iterated attic motives, and the girdling cornices are in another zone of experience. As the eye follows the curving wall and vault and it is apparent that this vast space is without corners, the spell of the design begins to work. There is really no place to *go*.[66]

This is ultimate space, "final architecture" that

> cannot be affected or interpreted by incidental human motion. It is too large to become a usable object, except perhaps as a container for ceremonies, too large to be readily digested by mental and sensory processes. There is no place to stand and become related to the surroundings, for in its general revelation the building is seamless.[67]

Sophisticated estrangement of space of this kind is perhaps unequaled elsewhere; but in a different way, in the domestic layout of the Alhambra in Granada, architecture achieves the displacement of common by divine volumes. The palace itself conventionally locates the ruler at the focus of an axial composition. But the succession of apartments violates Western conceptions of degree; as John Hoag has analyzed them, "vistas of successive spaces are tolerated only if they are repetitious . . . nonidentical spaces are so arranged that one cannot be seen from the other." The intent is to reproduce the *timelessness* of Paradise:

Since paradise is eternal, it may be that the curious method of space compartmentation here has symbolic value. A modulated series of successively changing spaces, frequent in Western architecture, implies the passage of time; but a series of identical spaces does not, nor does the abrupt transition from one to another. We may infer that Muhammad V, for his private apartments, chose to dwell in a timeless paradise. . . .[68]

As a model of "paradise" the Pantheon is, of course, not affected by biblical typologies, nor does it especially tempt our responsiveness to gold and jewels, much less to vernal airs. But the Pantheon represents in space the divorce from spatial and temporal limitations that otherwise govern the world, even Eden; and it is appropriate that the building is both an architectural dead end and a pointer to the subsequent, yet radically different, Hagia Sophia, designed to dominate Constantinople. The masterpiece of Justinian's architects, Anthemius of Tralles and Isidorus of Miletus, incorporates the engineering triumph of the pendentive, the curving triangle that bridges the gap between dome (or drum) and wall. From the freed spaces under the arches of the pierced walls radiate subsidiary chapels, aisles, and ambulatories, capable themselves of supporting domes. The space thus "discovered," in a happy term, is the more mysterious because the load-bearing piers are disguised by being nearly flush with the thin, pierced walls, reinforcing the illusion of weightlessness.[69] Interior space can thus be indefinitely expanded while processional axes for royal and liturgical affirmations of authority are maintained.

For it was in the East that the theological question of the nature of the kingdom of heaven tended to resolve itself into an identification of imperial with celestial regimes; Eusebius, the panegyrist who identified Constantine as the regent of Christ on earth, did not clearly distinguish between the empire and the Church,[70] and sacred relics pertaining to kingship, like the staff of Moses, were preserved at the palace.[71] As a type of the Temple of Solomon, Hagia Sophia qualified as much by virtue of the relics kept there—the tables of law, the ark of the Covenant—as by imitation of the ratios of the Temple chambers in length, width, and height. The synthesis of basilica and *tempietto* is thus a political triumph, as well as an architectural one, uniting the vertically axial, ceremonial dome of the god (here, the *basileus*, the theocratic emperor) with the horizontally axial Roman hall of assembly. As such, Hagia Sophia was both tool and symbol of the Byzantine state.

As heliocastron Hagia Sophia is a dome of heaven; the historian Procopius looked upward and maintained that the dome itself revolved. As a literary topos the great church is the subject of Paul the Silentiary's (died about A.D. 575) hexameter panegyric of the year 563, an architectural epic that describes the interior as a microcosm of the universe and that ranks with Francesco Colonna's fifteenth-century *Hypnerotomachia Poliphili* as a major rhapsody upon inert matter. Constantinople recurs in medieval literature in the West as an "otherworldly" place with architecture like that of heaven, or it appears domesticated for romance purposes, as, for example, in the "Besance" (Byzantium) where the hero of the anonymous twelfth-century *Partonopeus de Blois* finds himself. Perhaps the most singular example is the golden Constantinople of the anonymous eleventh-century(?) *Pèlerinage de Charlemagne*, in which Emperor Hugo lives in a vaulted palace that rotates when the wind blows—possibly an echo of Hagia Sophia and the legends surrounding it or of the imperial palace at Constantinople. Likening a dome or an interior to the vault of heaven was, in any case, a Byzantine and Islamic commonplace; a Syrian hymn of the sixth century forces the equation in the instance of a local church,[72] and the Alhambra palace of the eleventh cen-

29

Hagia Sophia dominating Constantinople,
from an engraving by George Sandys, from
his *A Relation of a Voyage Begun An: Dom:
1610*, 2nd ed., London, 1621.

30

Interior of Hagia Sophia, Constaninople,
from a nineteenth-century engraving by
Chevalier Fossatti, from his *Aya Sofia*,
London, 1852.

tury was praised for its supposedly rotating dome, perceived as both the palanquin of Solomon and as a chronometer harmonizing earth and sky.[73]

The Surface of Things

In preferring the Greek to the Latin cross, Renaissance architects, Rudolf Wittkower has suggested, replaced the Man of Sorrows with Christ Pantocrator in the general symbolism of ecclesiastical architecture.[74] The distinction between a penitential and a triumphant framework for celestial space implies a shift of emphasis from a postlapsarian to a presalvationist structure, the latter, in the finality of its perfect forms as defined by Alberti,[75] representing the celestial city more literally than the Gothic cathedral. In seeking to duplicate celestial space, the Gothic or Renaissance architect might rely on both the immaterial system of ratios and the cubic and rectangular volumes of the scriptural Temple, but in the identification of elevation, section, and plan as integrally interrelated in the scientific composition of the whole, the Renaissance artist was of necessity compelled to define the porportions (and thereby the elements to be proportioned) of the facades as well as of the hollows they confined, and, moreover, he had to define them as appropriate to the Temple. Scriptural exegesis in the sixteenth century had moved increasingly toward literalism, insisting on rationalistic historical inquiry to validate texts by means of precise chronology, geography, and in this case architecture. In insisting on propriety of elevation generally[76] and upon the rightness of Vitruvius in particular, theorists and architects invited a literal reconstruction of the Temple. The historical inevitability of the Vitruvian canon is caught in Pope's formula from the *Essay on Criticism* of 1711: "Those Rules of old *discover'd* not *devis'd*, / Are *Nature* still, but *Nature methodiz'd*."

Between 1596 and 1604 the Spanish Jesuits Jerónimo Prado and Juan Bautista Villalpando published three volumes of commentary on Ezekiel, with plates by Villalpando, extensively reconstructing the Temple of Solomon, which is identified with that of Ezekiel.[77] The project was subsidized by Philip II, to whom it was dedicated; the monarch counted "King of Jerusalem" among his titles, identified himself with Solomon[78] and intended his Escorial to be understood as a type of the Temple.[79] Villalpando grounded his Vitruvian reconstruction on the assumption that revelation does not contradict reason and that reason dictated that the Vitruvian canon constituted the only proper, the only possible, style for a divinely authorized structure. From Israel the Vitruvian orders passed to Greece and Rome.

In an elaborate allegorical interpretation of his vast plan, Villalpando identified various parts with the twelve tribes, the zodiac, the planets, and so on in a manner analogous to allegorical readings of the celestial Jerusalem. But his reconstruction succeeded anagogically rather than allegorically in conveying the mystical import of the great building; as René Taylor has observed, only by understanding the Temple in terms of *real* architecture can the perfection of the heavenly Jerusalem be understood.[80] At the same time only a complete model of the Temple could reconcile biblical authority with rational and mystical theories of harmonic proportion so that one might confidently equate Augustan and Renaissance architecture with what the sixteenth-century architect Philibert de l'Orme termed "les divines proportions venues du ciel."[81] Despite skirmishes and full-scale assaults from architects and theorists,[82] Villalpando's grandiose grid of nine courts and fifteen hundred columns continued to please well into the eighteenth century.[83] Subsequent reconstructions suggest not only classical tastes but also a craving for gigantism; in the 1720s both Bernard Lamy and Johann Fischer von Erlach published their versions, which follow Villalpando in transforming the sacred mount entirely into architecture.

31 and 32

Front and side elevations of the sanctuary
of the Temple of Solomon, as reconstituted
by Juan Bautista Villalpando in his and
Jerónimo Prado's lavish edition of
1596–1604, *In Ezechielem Explanationes et
Apparatus Urbis ac Templi Hierosolymitani*,
II, Rome. The Solomonic order, God's
own architecture, descends to us via Greece
and Rome in the fragmented systems–
Doric, Ionic, and so forth–of the
Vitruvian canon.

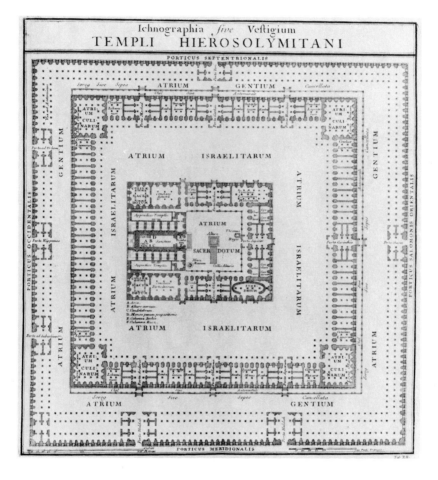

33 and 34

Plan and general view of the Temple
complex, by Bernard Lamy, from his *De
Tabernaculo Foederis, De Sancta Civitate
Jerusalem, et de Templo eius Libri Septem,*
Paris, 1720.

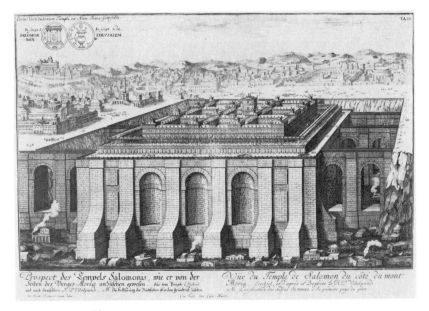

35

Johann Fischer von Erlach's contribution
to Temple imagery, from his *Entwürff einer
Historischen Architectur*, Leipzig, 1725.

36

Interior of the Holy of Holies, from
Jerónimo Prado and Juan Bautista
Villalpando, *In Ezechielem Explanationes et
Apparatus Urbis ac Templi Hierosolymitani*,
II, Rome, 1604.

37 and 38

Celestial symbolism at Nauvoo:
preliminary design for the temple by
William Weeks, mid-1840s; and a
capital detail, ca. 1847.

In detail as well, Villalpando's reconstruction united piety with rationality; the "sixth order" he composed for the Temple, a mélange of Doric and Corinthian, is supposed to be a unified prototype from which the five classical orders are descended. Motifs of palms, cherubim, and open flowers (1 Kings 6:29) appear in Villalpando's plates and may have directly influenced the Solomonic symbolism of Francesco Borromini's Sant'-Ivo alla Sapienza in Rome, designed in part to suggest that its ultimate patron, Alexander VII, was a type of Solomon.[84] "And I, Nephi, did build a temple," records the Book of Mormon (2 Nephi 5:16), "and I did construct it after the manner of the temple of Solomon." This was the temple erected in mythic times in America, for which the subsequent Mormon temples were replacements; the order of the Nauvoo temple incorporated symbolism of sun, moon, and stars, signifying the three realms, celestial, terrestrial, and telestial (Smith's mysterious category), prepared for the blessed. The neo-Solomonic order thus announced that the building was emblematic of heaven, and the way to get there as well.

The definition of the correct grammar of the facades of the temple is in one sense an extreme instance of the rematerialization of Paradise in the Renaissance, of that same movement from Aristotelian abstraction to Platonic corporeality that gives us Milton's flesh-and-blood angels instead of Aquinas's immaterial ones. By extension, not only Paradise but our own architectural environment may aspire to a correct language of forms: what is good for the temple must be good for other buildings. Villalpando's vision may appear narrowly materialistic and naïvely confined to the two dimensions of the temple's facades, but in its reduction of the celestial city to the detail of Vitruvian proportion and ornament, that system becomes immediately accessible and replicable. As a synthesis or reconciliation of divine and Roman architecture, it is, or could have been, the final style, the architecture of utopia, conferring on all mundane buildings the significance of the heavenly one.

PROPORTIONABLE RAPTURE

Ancient Poesy and ancient Architecture requiring to their excellence
a like creating and proportionable rapture. . . .

(GEORGE CHAPMAN, *Musaeus* [1616],
from the dedication to Inigo Jones)

Neither the reconstruction of the only divinely ordained building,
however, nor the merger of sacred and secular in the third Rome or in
any other city with eschatological pretensions has amounted to a
reversal of the moral tradition dismissive of architecture. There was
no common ground between these two ways of thinking until the
Renaissance when an understanding of architecture as an art imitative
of nature gained acceptance. In Augustus's time, Vitruvius had argued
for classifying architecture as one of the liberal arts, like oratory and
medicine; insisting on a foundation in theory, Vitruvius identified
architectural achievement with the physical and ecological demands of
structure and site, ultimately requiring conformity between architecture and the nature of man and the universe.[85] It is less in the
identification of architecture with nature, however, than in the redefinition of nature itself that Vitruvius laid a basis for the Renaissance glorification of the craft. In the manner of Lucretius's *De Rerum
Natura*, Vitruvius constructs a myth or parable of the origins of
building that does not depend upon the supernatural. Primitive man,
in his description (*De Architectura* II, 1), constructed shelters by
putting up unsquared timbers and interweaving them with branches;
divine aid is not suggested, nor is the act associated either with a sin
or with a spiritual lapse or failing. The "primitive hut" of his
rationalistic fable was a favorite subject of Renaissance writers on
architecture like Filarete (*Trattato d'Architettura*, 1470) and of illustrators of editions of *De Architectura*, from Jan Martin's edition of
1547 to Claude Perrault's of 1673. The primitive hut has nothing to

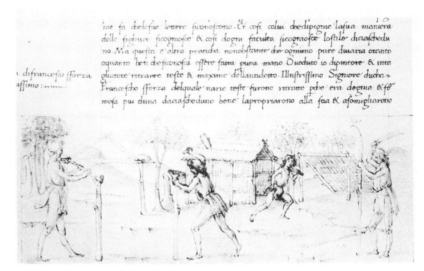

39 and 40

The first act of construction was a favorite
subject of Renaissance as well as classical
architectural theory. Illustrating the
rationalistic myth are Filarete, in his
Trattato d'Architettura, 1470 (facsimile
edition, New Haven: Yale University
Press, 1965); and Jean Goujon, in his
engraving from Jan Martin's French
edition of Vitruvius, *Architecture ou Art de
Bien Bastir*, Paris, 1547.

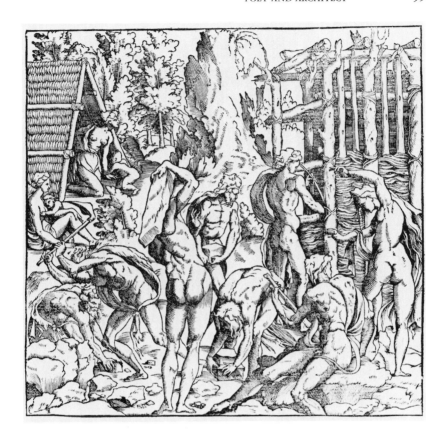

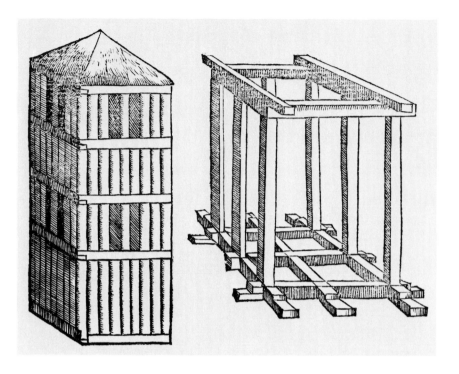

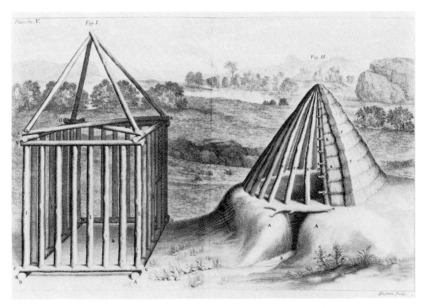

41 and 42

Reconstructions of prototypes of
architecture, from the French editions of
Vitruvius: Jan Martin, *Architecture ou Art
de Bien Bastir*, Paris, 1547; and Claude
Perrault, *Les dix livres d'architecture de
Vitruve*, Paris, 1673.

say to subsequent generations about how a building should be built; it is a document of the naturalness and necessity of the act of building and is the seed from which the craft of architecture will flower. In so defining construction as a natural act, Vitruvius differs from Seneca principally in that Seneca's version of human nature falls into two parts, divided by that primal lapse, whereas Vitruvius's is of a piece. In the quattrocento, only a slight accommodation to the Old Testament was needful in order to rationalize the first act of construction: "The first [postlapsarian] need and necessity of man, after food, was habitation; thus he endeavored to construct a place where he could dwell. From this, then, public and private buildings were derived. . . ."[86]

The architect, in Vitruvius's noble prescription, is a man of letters, liberally educated yet versed in law, medicine, and astronomy (*De Architectura* I, 1). He is the *uomo universale*, whom Alberti celebrates in the preface to his *De Re Aedificatoria* (ca. 1450) and whose profession, according to Palladio's patron Daniele Barbaro in the following century, most closely approaches the Platonic Idea. He likes to be known as a "lover of excellence" or as a heavenly spirit: Filarete [φίλος ἀρετῆς] and Palladio (after the goddess of wisdom, Pallas, who lent her name to a character in Giangiorgio Trissino's epic poem of 1547, *Italia liberata dai Goti*), are the significant pseudonyms of the architects Antonio Averlino and Andrea dalla Gondola. These men and others, like Leonardo da Vinci and Vincenzo Scamozzi, are the "moderns" in a quarrel that in literature appears in Renaissance translations of Homer, particularly in the passages on Alcinous's palace. James Yoch has shown how Chapman's first English edition of Homer ignored a moral tradition of hostile commentary on the supposed excess and viciousness of the decor in order to exaggerate with enthusiasm its material splendors.[87] In the court masques presented by Ben Jonson and Inigo Jones, the glories of poetic palaces are bodied forth in the sets, emblems of numinous royal authority;[88] in

43

Numinous royal authority bodied forth in
the set for the palace of Oceanus, from
Inigo Jones's masque *Neptune's Triumph*,
1624.

Chloridia, the last masque of the partnership, Architecture joins her sister arts as an attendant on Fame.

Jonson's cooperative spirit turned sour after 1631, and the famous quarrel between poet and architect has been understood as Jonson's defense of poetic content over architectural form—"painting and carpentry"—in the masque.[89] Perhaps the poets had been on safer ground in assuming the simply deprecatory stoic position of hostility to magnificence. Inigo Jones understood how both theatrical and real architecture comprehended the "content" of royal pretensions to divinity, and the court's vindication of him at the expense of Jonson, who then retired, is evidence that the moral and symbolic force of numinous architecture had reached a level of articulation to rival or exceed that of the literary representation of the craft of building.

THREE

Garden and City

A harmony of all the parts in whatsoever subject it appears,
fitted together with such proportion and connection, that
nothing could be added, diminished, or altered but for
the worse.

> (LEON BATTISTA ALBERTI, ca. 1450,
> *De Re Aedificatoria*, VI, 2: definition of beauty)

TWO PARADISES

The left panel of Fra Angelico's *The Last Judgment* in Florence shows
us the double image of Paradise fixed in literature since Claudian's
Epithalamium on Emperor Honorius Augustus. Two icons are side by
side, garden and city, the latter enclosed by the former, and each
proffers a distinct order of beatitude. The bastioned city satisfies as a
representation of triumph, power, and security, the garden as a
representation of innocent delights; but their juxtaposition is irra-
tional. Between security and play there is a disjunction; if security lies
within the walls, then the outlying park is vulnerable; if the park is
not vulnerable, then the walls and the city are superfluous.

Milton may or may not have known this painting or others like it,[1]
showing the blessed at play before the celestial ramparts, but the
scheme of heaven in *Paradise Lost* transcends the ambiguity; the
pattern of heaven is echoed in Eden and inverted in hell. Correspon-
dences among the several realms of the poem are of course numerous

44

The saved celebrate in the celestial garden
beneath the ramparts of the city, Fra
Angelico, *The Last Judgment*, left panel,
ca. 1430.

and have been often pursued, but the physical analogies, though important, depend upon a consistent double vision that presents images of Paradise in the light both of unfallen and of fallen knowledge. Raphael teases Adam by asking rhetorically,

> what if Earth
> Be but the shaddow of Heav'n, and things therein
> Each t'other like, more then on earth is thought?
> (V, 574–76)

His tentative equation resonates throughout the poem because both heaven and earth (and hell too) are arenas of process, where choice, not certainty, determines conduct. Only God is outside of time, and the force of his challenge to the heavenly host to be a sacrifice for mankind—"Dwels in all Heaven charitie so dear?" (III, 216)— depends upon a consciousness among angels as much as among men of the unknowability of the future, of the consequent progressive and irreversible nature of time, and of the moral significance of willed action.

The celestial city embodies the consciousness of history, of process, and of threat; it achieves perfection at the sacrifice of timeless bliss; it is the cockpit of history. We know it as the triumphant but depopulated arena of a great struggle. The garden is its counterpart in that there, also, liberty and innocence are maintained behind a defensive wall, both natural and military. There, also, process, time, and history are integrated into innocent human experience, most especially in the parallel educations of Adam by Raphael and of Eve by Adam. Eden is always in a state of change. Milton's city of God likewise is meaningful to us and to the angels and to Messiah, only within the framework of the perilous historical time that begins at Messiah's unveiling and ends beyond our ken, when "God shall be All in All" (III, 341).

It is not necessary or inevitable, though it might appear to be so, that Milton present the garden in the context of future events; his Virgilian regrets woven into the descriptions of unfallen man and nature occur after both we, Messiah, and the heavenly host have been told by God what is to happen (III, 92ff.), and so the "timeless" experience of prelapsarian Paradise is yoked to the time-bound one of postlapsarian knowledge. This is not only the knowledge of one's own fallen nature; it is also knowledge of the Fall as a fact in the nature of others and involves the good angels, whose knowledge of their erstwhile companions' fall has already entrained them in the mechanism of historical time—in which, of course, they have participated by putting on the whole armor of God.

The iconographies and topographies of heaven, the garden, and hell are complex accommodations of the double perspective that permits us to understand the timeless, self-renewing qualities of Paradise within the context of the historical time of the epic; the larger, inverse problem, of understanding the time-bound within the framework of the timeless, is the matter of God's and Michael's discursive speeches. As an equivalent—in an Aristotelian sense—of perfection, timelessness is inherent in the material structures and organizations of both paradisal realms, which are however both fashioned with a view toward repelling agents of pejorative change. The woody wall of the earthly paradise is thus a major elaboration of Genesis, though consecrated by literary tradition; it finds its place within a series of filled and therefore fulfilled spaces within which, as a critic has noted, Milton's universe is to some extent organized.[2] They descend from the girdle of the "seat of bliss" (VI, 273) through the self-enclosing planetary spheres, to the "woodie Theatre / Of stateliest view" (IV, 141-42). Here is imitated Virgil's picture of the bay near Carthage: *tum silvis scaena coruscis / desuper*, "then overhead there is a wall of waving woods" (*Aeneid* I, 164-65); *scaena* literally means the wall of a theater, and the architectural image is latent in Milton's natural barrier.[3]

Milton's heaven is rich in urban elements, all of them probably connected with the walls. Mulciber had erected "many a Towred structure high, /Where Scepter'd Angels held their residence" (I, 733-34); and because towers recur in conjunction with the walls and other components of the fortifications ("doors" and "battlements" are mentioned often; the first sight of heaven is of walls "With Opal Towrs and Battlements adorn'd" [II, 1049]), these proconsular seats may plausibly make up part of them. Satan's palace lies, for example, in "the limits of the North" (V, 755). The presence of elaborate architectural elements, then, does not obstruct our perception of the essentially nomadic quality of angelic life, hardly pastoral in a Virgilian sense but like that of the Hebrews in the desert:

> Wide over all the Plain, and wider farr
> Then all this globous Earth in Plain outspred,
> (Such are the Courts of God) th'Angelic throng
> Disperst in Bands and Files thir Camp extend
> By living Streams among the Trees of Life,
> Pavilions numberless, and sudden reard,
> Celestial Tabernacles. . . .
>   (V, 648-54)

Here the angels might truly say:

> Within this holy leisure, we
> Live innocently, as you see.
> These walls restrain the world without,
> But hedge our Liberty about.[4]

The paradox that was central to Marvell's earlier (ca. 1652) praise of a Yorkshire estate is appropriate for the same reason to Milton's heaven; both demesnes are located within the context of history and are to be distinguished from an inferior or even hostile "world without": "the Towrs of Heav'n are fill'd / With armed watch" (II, 129–30) who make military sorties into the void.

It is less than complete, then, to contrast a pastoral or timeless heaven to the urban dystopia of hell;[5] and to decry the architecture of Pandaemonium as "artificial" and consequently as "superficial, . . . extrinsic, and counterfeit"[6] begs the question of the merit of architecture, or of the use of precious materials, by identifying the act of building or the achieved work with the character of the builder.[7] It is equally question begging to explain away architectural splendors by arguing that "the brilliance of Heaven has nothing to do with human estimates of value; these (the walls [II, 1049–50; III, 504–08]) are simply the finest, and purest, materials conceivable."[8] What is this if not a human estimate? Yet in another sense this statement is right. The combination of natural with artificial in the descriptive language of *Paradise Lost* has been a subject of criticism for centuries. The significance both of architecture and of inorganic nature in *Paradise Lost* arises from the distinct kinds of metaphorical language used to describe the two Paradises.

At the center of the celestial landscape is the mount of God, mysteriously described as a temple (VI, 890; VII, 148), with rites like those of the temple on earth; it is also called God's house (VII, 576). In the Psalms, "mountain" and "temple" are interchangeable terms, as Michael Murrin has pointed out, "and the Temple ritual itself was instituted and first performed on Mt. Sinai."[9] In perpetuating this blurred visual image, Milton sets up the first term in a series of calculated ambiguities in which natural and artificial structures, and organic and inorganic nature, are conflated. This is true both of heaven and of Eden, but in a different way.

Our overview of heaven is paradoxical; it is "undetermind square or round" (II, 1048).[10] Paradox continues through sapphire that lives (II, 1050), vines fruitful of pearl, diamond, and gold (V, 633–35), a sea "Of Jasper, or of liquid Pearl" (III, 518–19), to an immortal flower the name of which (*amaranth*, "unfading"), as D. C. Allen has observed, conveys neither color nor form;[11] the flower is watered by an "Amber stream" and woven with gold into angelic coronets (III, 352ff.), where it remains unfading. Superficially, the ambiguities are the same as those found in details of Eden, like "vegetable Gold" (IV, 220), where organic and inorganic nature appear to be synthesized. But as Murrin has shown, the landscape of heaven is distanced to a greater degree from our sensuous apprehension by a series of qualifying ambivalencies: We are asked to see a pavement "of Jasper, *or* of liquid Pearl" or to notice that it shone "*like* Jasper"; the indefiniteness is part of Raphael's acknowledged rhetorical strategy intended to "relate / To human sense th'invisible" (V, 564–65), a difficult task because the matter of heaven is "inaccessible even to unfallen human sense,"[12] and we are prevented from human estimates of value.

Adam, then, might well have had difficulty in figuring to his inner eye the "bright/Pavement that like a Sea of Jasper shon/Impurpl'd with Celestial Roses" (III, 362–64), where colors impossibly fuse, and the reflection of a glittering pavement is united to the soft density of a surface of petals. In perceiving his garden, we are to him as he is to Raphael. Despite the lack of estranging ambivalencies of language, the garden where nature is a synthesis of the organic and the inorganic taxes our capacities for sensuous apprehension. Typically, "vegetable Gold" is a phrase of two nouns, each of which may be taken as an adjective, but it is impossible to prefer one to the other. We can neither insist upon the literalness of the metal in the fruit nor reject it as metaphor; it is living gold, an aureated apple. What is difficult for us is presumably not difficult for unfallen senses, and even for us it is not impossible; like the statue in *The Winter's Tale*, gold that lives "would beguile nature of her custom," but what cannot be explained may be accepted, and what is taken on faith, though obscure in its causes, is unambiguous in its manifestation. How heaven manifests its physical nature is certainly ambiguous to us; perhaps it would have been less so to unfallen human senses. In any case, it is not the "what" but the "how" that is unanswerable in the description of Eden:

> But rather to tell how, if Art could tell
> How from that Saphire Fount the crisped Brooks,
> Rowling on Orient Pearl and sands of Gold . . .
> Ran Nectar. . . .
>
>   (IV, 236–38, 240)

In heaven we understand a union of polarities; in Eden these unified polarities appear in the form of the synthesis of organic and inorganic nature, each transferring to the other its characteristic virtue of vitality, or permanence; but in reascending to heaven by way of Raphael's narrative, we are warned either that the synthesis up there is of materials more complex or that the nature of the synthesis is more complex.

We may be confident, however, that the descriptive language of Eden, even if less than adequate, is appropriate to heaven; Raphael's definition of his own narrative technique, "lik'ning spiritual to corporal forms" (V, 573), implies an anagogical and therefore sensuously significant relationship between the two realms. As we may be sure of heaven's natural richness, with meadows of jasper fused with roses, where dew is "pearly grain" (V, 430), and where the tree of life is multiplied into groves of indefinite extension (V, 652), so we may also be certain of the solid presence of its crafted elements. They are literally rooted in the soil of heaven because inorganic phenomena are not distinguished from organic:

> Which of us who beholds the bright surface
> Of this Ethereous mould whereon we stand,
> This continent of spacious Heav'n, adornd
> With Plant, Fruit, Flowr Ambrosial, Gemms and Gold,
> Whose Eye so superficially surveys
> These things, as not to mind from whence they grow
> Deep under ground. . . .
>
>   (VI, 472–78)

Heaven is not only a place where precious, inorganic nature finds full validation in a mysterious synthesis with its contrary; it is the place where that synthesis achieves architectural expression. The dichotomy between battlements and meadows is muted by the transposition of the enduring nature of one into the vital nature of the other, but both are affirmed as distinct, complementary components of heaven. By contrast, precious metals unmodified by organic language (as "living," "vegetable") are frequently sterile in a moral as well as generative sense. As Isabel MacCaffrey has pointed out, the sun is composed of splendid, precious metals (III, 594–97), but "barren shines / Whose vertue on it self works no effect, / But in the fruitful Earth" (VIII, 94–96).[13] Satan's palace in heaven conspicuously lacks any organic modifier, in this defect resembling Pandaemonium; the walls "of living Saphire" (II, 1050), which roll inward to cooperate with Messiah's climactic push of the rebels out of heaven, are by contrast not only sentient but, however briefly, moral creatures.

In Eden, the union of organic and inorganic achieves its most complex expression in the world's unique structure, the bower. Both as a dwelling, deriving from the Old English *búr*, and as a bedroom, a sense it has had since before the Norman Conquest, and as a secluded area in a grove (elsewhere "the unpierc't shade / Imbrownd the noontide Bowrs" [IV, 245–46]), the carefully chosen noun obliges us to conflate a natural with a constructed shelter. Again Milton elides the literal with the metaphorical:

> the roof
> Of thickest covert was inwoven shade
> Laurel and Mirtle, and what higher grew
> Of firm and fragrant leaf; on either side
> *Acanthus*, and each odorous bushie shrub
> Fenc'd up the verdant wall; each beauteous flowr,
> *Iris* all hues, Roses, and Gessamin
> Rear'd high thir flourisht heads between, and wrought
> Mosaic; underfoot the Violet,
> Crocus, and Hyacinth with rich inlay

> Broiderd the ground, more colour'd then with stone
> Of costliest Emblem . . .
>
> (IV, 692–703)

Here living nature is not merely synthesized with the nonliving but assimilated to the crafts in which inorganic nature is fulfilled: roofing, walling, and flooring expressed as embroidery and mosaic; the acanthus is the leaf of the Corinthian column.[14] Architecture and her attendant crafts are present here in unity with nature, "implied" in the Miltonic sense of "wrapped together" in the nature from which they have not become separated. J. B. Broadbent is partly right in observing that "τέχνη, art, though now conventionally and with wide ethical implications opposed to φύσις, nature, must then have been inherent in nature,"[15] yet the force of the synthesis goes beyond what is suggested by comparisons to the garden of Adonis, where nature merely behaves artistically, or conveniently (there, *The Faerie Queene*, III, vi, 44, the bower is "not by art / But of the trees owne inclination made"). By suppressing terms of comparison and by stressing the ineluctability and independence of inorganic phenomena, like "mosaic," Milton invites us to understand a τέχνη coequal with φύσις and fully developed rather than latent within the synthesis, or fusion. Two of William Blake's illustrations for *Paradise Lost* show a rare understanding of the vital architectonics of the bower, which in art has been conventionally ignored or rendered as a grove, a cave, or some ambiguous form or mass.[16]

"It was a place / Chos'n by the sovran Planter" (IV, 690–91), and the loss of it is equivalent to the loss of that race of unfallen men at whose head, with the passing of obedient years, Adam and Eve were to stand (IV, 732–34). Wedded love, Milton says, is the "sole proprietie, / In Paradise of all things common else" (IV, 751–52), and the high decorum of their sexuality demands private space. We remain outside as the pair go "into thir inmost bowr / Handed" (IV, 738–39); the intimacy of enclosed space is intensified by language such as "inwoven shade," "fenc'd up," "sacred and sequesterd," and "close recess." The garden, whose abundance requires their constant pruning, is by contrast "this delicious place / For us too large" (IV, 729–30). Both spatially, because it is their center of Paradise—they are "Imparadis't in one anothers arms" (IV, 506)—and temporally, because it not only is but has been there for an indefinite length of time, nearly "forever," the bower makes Eden probable for us. Philo Judaeus asked why the likeness of Eve is a building (ὀικοδομήν) and answered, "The harmonious coming together of man and woman is figuratively a house."[17] It is the fixed abode, *certa domus*, that distinguishes their fruitful participation in a benevolently progressive time from the timelessness of literary arcadias.

Milton's two Paradises correspond to each other in their mutual accommodation of the three offices of the conventional paradisal day, rest, feast, and the sight of God.[18] If heaven is hortulan to the point of outdoor camping and alfresco entertainments, so Eden is formal in including the rituals of morning and evening song. The polarities of the saints who rest in Eden and the righteous who rejoice in Jerusalem are modified, though not discarded; both Eden and heaven are syntheses of arcadian and utopian programs. Each departs from its model—the Yahwist garden, the city of the apocalypse—moving toward the other along a shared axis of metaphorical language. Each is a garden-city where antagonistic or insoluble phenomena—living and nonliving nature, nature and craft—are reconciled and dissolved one into the other. Each maintains a relative degree of polarity with regard to the other by the predominant position of its original model; so in heaven nature is assimilated to a city, in Eden a house is assimilated to a garden.

Overriding the brief and precarious state of balance between the two Paradises, however, is the dynamic movement of history that seeks to return the garden, or the condition of bliss it makes possible, to the more sophisticated arena of the heavenly city, the model from which Eden was derived. The reader of *Paradise Lost* knows that the

45 and 46

Alone among the illustrators of John
Milton's *Paradise Lost*, William Blake
expresses the living architecture of the
bower, in walling, flooring, and furniture
synthesizing nature and craft, ca. 1808.

garden is doomed from the start; he never knows of the beginning or end, if any, of the heavenly city. Consequently, what Milton makes available in his epic is the "prologue" to Genesis conspicuously lacking in the Bible, viewed synoptically; time's movement is circular, from city to garden to city. Northrop Frye has argued at length that William Blake's epic visions of paradise lost and regained depend upon just such an urbane vision of civilized or perfect human existence. Eden is a sunlit city, an image of the fiery city of Revelation; all creative and imaginative acts, which are eternal, serve to build the city of Golgonooza, which will ultimately become the New Jerusalem, "the total form of all human culture and civilization."[19]

Primitive Huts

In giving Adam and Eve a house, Milton contributed to a mythology of ideal primitivist construction that was to be most clearly formulated in the following centuries. The bower in Eden is the extreme example of a work of architecture legitimized by its integration with nature and can exist only as a literary construction. But in the quest for right architecture the primitive hut may claim to have been "*right* because it was *first*";[20] those seeking to reconstruct it deny, with Seneca, the right of the imagination to modify nature to accord with conceptual ends and share the stoic and georgic admiration for architecture that departs little or not at all from the appearances and functions of its raw materials. The primitive hut may claim to be the only necessary architecture, the equivalent for man of the bird's nest or the tortoise's shell. As such it is in its purest forms an architecture of very limited compromise: the Senecan antagonism to craft is compromised by the toleration of craft considered faithful to the nature that craft generally profanes.

The quest for the primitive hut is a search for an art that in Aristotle's sense completes or fulfills nature, without violating her;

and as a literary enterprise that search emanates from stoic disparage-
ment of craft in favor of rude savagery. The suave translations of these
principles into the praise of Roman villas and English country houses
have been my subject elsewhere.[21] The characteristics of a "natural
house" within country-house poems and related genres—those of
Horace's "Happy Man" or Virgil's farmers—are antiarchitectural; the
buildings are purged, neutralized architecture. Writing to praise a
farm and slander a villa, Martial (*Epigrams*, Book III, 58) is specific
about the appearance of the latter, indifferent to that of the former;
it remains for us to assume that, like the Penshurst of Ben Jonson's related poem, it stands "an ancient pile." The displacement of
material by moral structures, the priority given the virtuous content
over the presumably vicious form even of a good house, governs
Andrew Marvell's eulogy on Appleton House, which refers us to
George Wither's popular emblem of a tortoise before a country cottage, types of proper accommodation:

> Why should of all things man unrul'd
> Such unproportion'd dwellings build?
> The beasts are by their dens exprest,
> And birds contrive an equal nest;
> The low roof'd Tortoises do dwell
> In cases fit of Tortoise-shell:
> No creature loves an empty space;
> Their bodies measure out their place.[22]

The plan and elevation of Appleton House, the "sober frame" so
appropriate to the virtuous master of the estate, Lord Fairfax, are
never visible to us; more distinct is the "marble crust" of a vainglori-
ous rival structure, "Whose Columnes should so high be rais'd / To
arch the Brows that on them gaz'd" (lines 7–8). It is within this
reflexive literary stance that Pope writes in his epistles to Richard
Boyle, Earl of Burlington of 1731 and to Allen, Lord Bathurst of
1732, similarly discounting baroque architectural extravagance in

favor of a mysterious and unrealistic bucolic ideal that superimposes the image of the virtuous farmer of the Roman republic upon that of the aristocrat guided by strict Palladian principles of country-house construction.

Natural Artifacts

In juxtaposing a tortoise to a cottage as functional equivalents, the emblematist George Wither effectively extended the definition of nature to an artifact, insofar as that artifact (the cottage) qualified as wholly or essentially "natural" by virtue of perceived submission to natural laws (like the shell, it is a perfect fit) or by virtue of the unaltered nature of its materials (which refer us without distortion to their source in nature) or insofar as it could be understood as the equivalent or complement of the "content," or virtuous life led within. These are the formulas by which architecture overcomes or circumvents the classical moral strictures against craft, for these are the terms on which architecture is ethically permissible. The routes of translation from the literary assumptions of Jonson, Marvell, or Pope to the rhetoric of modernist architectural ideology are various and elaborate, but two instances may serve to demonstrate the process of modification and adaptation that has kept the tortoise and the cottage useful as metaphors of functionalist theory.

Literary tradition in the English Renaissance remained faithful to its Latin models in deducing relatively primitive architectural forms from a given basis of moral content; whatever the actual sophistication of a virtuous (or at least acceptable) building, it had to meet criteria of identity with "nature," understood as essential and the equivalent of the building's content, just as "art" was the equivalent of its form. But to discover an essential "moral," "right," or "natural" form antecedent to content would turn the situation on its head: desirable content, rather than determining form, would flow from it.

47

A tortoise and a country cottage are both
perfectly fitted, form to content,
inner life to outward manifestation,
engraving from George Wither's
A Collection of Emblemes, 1635.

That form emerges in the eighteenth century in consequence of French rationalistic inquiry into the nature of the orders.[23] In his *Essai sur l'architecture* of 1753, the Jesuit Marc-Antoine Laugier, eager to legitimize neoclassicism as the only proper style, derived from his own rationalistic account of the construction of the first, "primitive" wooden hut the language of column, entablature, and pediment. The hut has not, in the frontispiece to the 1755 edition, even ceased to be "nature," inasmuch as the upright members are still rooted in the earth. From this prototype derive *toutes les magnificences de l'architecture*, not in the conventional evolutionary sense set forth by Vitruvius (*De Architectura* II, 1) and accepted in Laugier's time, that the first construction was the germ of all future building, but in the radical sense that the first construction, as a necessary and natural and inevitable act, held formal authority as a model for all subsequent acts of building.[24]

The Senecan question—Should it have been built?—is submerged in the analysis of how it must have been built; and by referring unfailingly to it, the modern architect, regardless of the materials he uses, avoids error and conforms to nature's laws. What is not implied by the three structural elements, such as a wall, is tolerated if it fulfills minimally necessary functions and without flourish. What is neither implicit in column, entablature, or pediment nor necessary to the purposes of the building—pilasters, for example—is forbidden. An ideal building is the Maison Carrée at Nîmes; here the language of the Corinthian order is not expressive of a solidity in the building it decorates but in fact constitutes that solidity. The order is the building.

Structures of this kind are identifiable with nature because they repeat a primal act and because they allow no disjunction between form and content or hollow and shell. They cannot be neutralized in the conventional literary manner. The negative formulas of poetry permitted architecture to assimilate itself to nature through identity of materials and through echoes of natural forms. What Laugier authorizes is the reverse: to assimilate nature to architecture by locating the quintessentially natural act of construction within a vocabulary of specific structural relationships. The ethical validation for architecture remains the same–that architecture conforms to "nature"–but the restriction to prosaic materials or to materials disposed in imitation of natural forms (like the snug cottage that mimics the turtle's shell) dissolves into the liberating form of an architectural language that is an abstraction, not identifiable with wood or stone alone, and that imitates a primal act that is conceptual and willed rather than instinctual and reflexive.

Quarrels about propriety of architectural design do not begin in the Enlightenment, but it is then, and especially in Laugier, that arguments from beyond the discipline of architecture–from ethics, from religion–are formally divorced from the question of where virtue in design resides. If it is to structural design itself, rather than to the "content" or "function" of a building, that we look for an ethical validation of architecture, then the field is open for competition for the laurels of the only proper style. The history of architecture for two centuries has reflected that competition. Gothic architecture, for example, could be construed and advanced as the outgrowth of natural forms, or the primal architectural act could be the creation of the pointed arch. It was within this climate of theoretical rigor that Ruskin denounced Palladio's architecture as empty of moral content;[25] modern architecture is born out of such discriminations.

The Rehabilitation of Luxury

The effect of Laugier's reformulation of the structure of architecture's relationship to nature is that the problem of luxury is redefined as the problem of function. Classical hostility to architecture normally took the form of general antagonism to luxury in its widest sense: anything unneeded. But redefinition of luxury not as mere superfluity

48

The goddess *Architectura* points to the
first, authoritative structure, from the
frontispiece to Marc-Antoine Laugier's
Essai sur l'architecture, 2nd edition, 1755.

49

The order is the building: The Maison
Carrée (ca. 20–15 B.C.), Nîmes, the
embodiment of Marc-Antoine Laugier's
architectural idealism, is a sophisticated
primitive hut in an engraving by
Charles-Louis Clérisseau (1722–1820).

50

Eugène Emmanuel Viollet-le-Duc's
rationalistic proto-Gothic first hut, from
the American edition, 1876, of his
Histoire de l'habitation humaine.

but as a violation of the essential nature of a being or thing was implicit in classical moralizing. Plutarch records in his life of the Spartan Lycurgus (a Stoic prototype):

It was because he was used to . . . simplicity that Leotychides the Elder, as we are told, when he was dining in Corinth, and saw the roof of the house adorned with costly panelings, asked his host if trees grew square in that country.[26]

Although the wit is provincial, the point is that "luxury" is a question not of waste but of the order or fitness of things. Leotychides implies that a properly paneled ceiling would preserve or restate the natural forms of the trees or that the coffers would be acceptable were trees actually square. The objection is not to panels as such—an apparent "luxury"—but to their form.

Luxury as a *formal* vice in a building lies at the heart of the rhetoric of modernist ideology, of what has been called by Sigfried Giedion "the demand for morality in architecture."[27] In the American context that gave birth to Louis Sullivan and Frank Lloyd Wright, that "demand" will make most sense in the wider picture of nineteenth-century calls for purification in private morals and public institutions. In architecture Horatio Greenough had presciently called for a reformation of architectural ornament, "to arrest the tide of sensuous and arbitrary embellishment," while giving shape to the idea that would emerge as the cliché of modernism:

Instead of forcing the function of every sort of building into one general form, adopting an outward shape for the sake of the eye of association, without reference to the inner distribution, let us begin from the heart as a nucleus, and work outward.[28]

Greenough's words are noted and extended in *Walden*, of which Thoreau devotes a substantial part of the first chapter, "Economy," to

51 and 52

Naturally Gothic: Nature's behavior is
pointedly artistic, as well as architecturally
pointed. Primitive construction looks
backward to the behavior of the living
wood, and forward to the arch and
quatrefoil, in illustrations from the
frontispiece and Plate XI of Sir James
Hall's *Essays on the Origins, History, and
Principles of Gothic Architecture*, 1813.

the subject of architecture. But it is the unique status of *Walden* in American letters as a manifesto of liberation at once hedonistic and severely puritanical that gives his architectural observations so much force. Thoreau agreed with Greenough that contemporary architecture failed to unite form to content, or appearances to functions, but he dismissed Greenough's concentration on propriety of style, placing his emphasis rather on the moral character that must precede and determine any style:

> What of architectural beauty I now see, I know has gradually grown from within outward, out of the necessities and character of the indweller, who is the only builder—out of some unconscious truthfulness, and nobleness, without ever a thought for appearance; and whatever additional beauty of this kind is destined to be produced will be preceded by a like unconscious beauty of life.[29]

Thoreau had his own "country house," the famous hut at Walden Pond, and in his writings he describes several other structures. The architecture in each case is moralized and anthropomorphic; the famous and fussy itemizations of the materials and costs of construction for the Walden hermitage are more than the "economies" celebrated throughout the chapter, and more than exempla of frugality against luxury, in its sense of superfluity. They are intimacies, identifications of his body and its needs with the protective shell of the house, "this frame, so lightly clad, a sort of crystallization around me" (p. 85). In expanding on Greenough's arguments, he calls for a house "whose inside is as open and manifest as a bird's nest" (p. 244) and elsewhere describes the structure of a lodge in Maine, whose logs

> were held one upon another by very large pins, driven in diagonally on each side, where branches might have been and then cut off so close up and down as not to project beyond the bulge of the log, as if the logs clasped each other in their arms.[30]

53

A sketch of the hut at Walden Pond,
from the title page of the first
edition of *Walden*, 1854.

The house is both a tree and a loving couple; details of construction are approved to the extent that they correspond to the original structure of the materials (for example, logs mimic the position of branches); and the building is merely an extension of nature, "so primitive that you could at once refer it to its source . . . but a slight departure from the hollow tree, which the bear still inhabits, being a hollow made up with trees piled up, with a coating of bark, like its original."[31] Elsewhere in *Walden* he celebrates

a larger and more populous house, standing in a golden age, of enduring materials, and without gingerbread work, which shall consist of only one room, a vast, rude substantial primitive hall, without ceiling or plastering, with bare rafters and purlins supporting a sort of lower heaven over one's head. (p. 243)

With its single room, "enduring materials," and continuity between inner and outer surfaces of the shell (in the prohibition of a ceiling or of plaster), this imagined structure is a material metaphor for unity and the transcendence of time.

The Senecan argument against all craft has seemed disturbing in the light of the more accepted stoical appreciation of the dignity of labor. Although united in their antagonism to luxury, the pastoral or savage moralist who imagines a life free of both work and desire and the georgic poet or memorialist of country life are natural antagonists. It is here that Thoreau's linkage of architecture to personal character departs from the antique and accepted mode of opposition to luxury, for in his refusal to play the Horatian husbandman as much as in his rejection of mercantile and professional activities, Thoreau begs the question of "content" or "function" in his own life. It is as functionless as the Senecan unfallen man's, and as free. The key to the perennial popularity of *Walden* among American youth, and indeed to its status as perhaps the greatest national meditation, lies in its

Senecan synthesis of restraint and release, of self-denial and absolute freedom of choice. The model to be imitated – Thoreau's own life – is a structural prototype, a parable or fable, and not a specific pattern of behavior or set of actions to be duplicated.

The same is true of his architecture, whose radical primitivism is carefully associated with his own choices in life and which he will allow to be supplanted by "architecture" in its more formal sense should the ordinary citizen ever achieve a life "simple and agreeable to the imagination." The question of specifically proper "content" – of the life, for example, of the Horatian farmer – is irrelevant; only the knowledge of the self and of the universe, Seneca's prescription for the philosophic life in *Moral Epistle* 90, constitutes "content" or "function" in experience. As no man's life can be prescribed, so no architectural forms can be predetermined; the limitation placed on the form of a structure is implicitly only the restriction to proper expression of its in-dweller's "beautiful living." Doubtless for Thoreau the beauty of life that alone would bring about beautiful architecture would never have extended far beyond a life of material simplicity and restraint; but he left the door open for anyone to define the matter for himself. In implying that the form of a structure is legitimized by its conformity to beautiful living within and in refraining from prescribing that living, Thoreau sets no limits for the architect. Like Laugier, he locates architecture's conformity to nature in its faithful expression of function, and unlike him he infuses the concept of function with powerful and ambiguous moralizing on the integrity of the self and the irreplaceable and unique character of individual experience. The two constitute an index to the moral authority to which modern architecture has pretended: the authority of internal structural relationships over external demands of function, and the authority of the unique and ever-new solution to every architectural problem, the unique and ever-new expressive form for every individual function. Both Laugier's hut and Thoreau's are codes capable of infinite expansion; their descendants in modern architecture need claim only to have followed nature by expressing function through form to appropriate their legitimate status.

Modern architecture owes much to Laugier's reversal of the primary status of "content," but it has flourished with the neutralizations of the classical injunctions against luxury in its sense of superfluity. As a violation of the building's true nature rather than as a characteristic of the life of the inhabitant—that is, as a question of purely architectural morality—luxury, or excess, or even its equivalent modernist term "falsehood," is no threat to the architect, who is held to no particular model of virtuous living or function in the determination of proper form but only to the logic of the form itself. The power of the functionalist formula, which identifies both "nature" and "virtue" in architecture as the equivalence of a structure with its contents, lies in its adaptability to shifting definitions of "nature." What the rhetorical, metaphorical tradition insists upon is continuity—between interior and exterior, being and seeming, content and form, life and architecture. What is actually approved varies from the hollow of a tree to a lodge, a farm, an ancient manor, a spruce Palladian villa, a prairie house, or a glass tower.

MACHINES FOR LIVING

The metaphor governing advanced architecture of the nineteenth and twentieth centuries is the equivalence of man and house, and it joins the literary to the architectural history of forms. Augustus Welby Pugin, Eugène Viollet-le-Duc, William Lethaby, and Ebenezer Howard share with John Ruskin as well as with Greenough and Thoreau the conception of architecture as the exteriorization of the moral nature of men and (except for Thoreau) the conviction that it is a mechanism for realizing that nature. The eclectic competitions of

the nineteenth century amount to a pursuit of the timeless; this quest
is a chapter in the historical movement defined by Karl Popper:

the historicist believes . . . that by contemplating history we may
discover the secret, the essence of human destiny. Historicism is out
to find The Path on which mankind is destined to walk; it is out to
discover The Clue to History, or the Meaning of History.[32]

David Watkin has related holistic thought of this kind to Sigfried
Giedion, whose *Space, Time, and Architecture* "is inspired by a belief
that some universally acceptable synthesis, some permanent modern
consensus, is just around the corner."[33] Pernicious or fructifying, the
functionalist formula has served to neutralize the conflict between
ethics and architecture by expanding ethical architecture to the limits
of the materially possible.

The union in modern theory of architectural form and content has
been felt to be a spiritual triumph, and the architecture resulting from
that union has presented itself in a cloud of paradisal rhetoric. The
credo of the modernist movement has been the reformation and
rejuvenation of society; the model for the life to come combines
arcadian and utopian programs. States of grace and ecstasy implicit
respectively in the archetypes of Eden and Jerusalem descend into the
tranquil *otium* of the arcadian vision and into the fruitful labors of the
utopian. Modern architecture and planning attempt syntheses of the
two, perhaps tentatively in the suburban garden-cities of Ebenezer
Howard, more explicitly and with immensely greater influence in Le
Corbusier's *ville radieuse* and in Frank Lloyd Wright's Broadacre City.

The rhetoric in both cases is holistic and eschatological; the two
men are linked by the bond of their shared metaphor of architecture as
conformable to nature, and in Le Corbusier's typical exaltation of the
machine and in Wright's romantic naturalism the polarizing definitions of "nature" are seen. Construction for each is a moral act, by

virtue in Wright's case of being gathered to natural rhythms, by virtue in the instance of Le Corbusier of gathering natural forms to itself (the distinction merits analysis of the kind Heinrich Wölfflin, in *The Sense of Form in Art*, applies to painting, sculpture, and architecture as imitative either of spatial or of temporal phenomena). As polemicists, both argue for an architecture of humanism, with all proportions keyed to the scale of the body[34] but embracing their immediate humanistic intentions are the larger models of garden and city.

That both Wright's "organic" and Le Corbusier's "mechanistic" metaphors for buildings proceed from a unified conception of the relationship of art to nature and of form to function is explicit in Greenough's division of the term "organic" into two categories: natural, as in the bodies of animals, and mechanical, as in a ship.[35] Both are appropriate models for architecture; both are redemptive. So Wright's rhetoric is as religious as it is naturalistic; he calls his architectural text "the book of creation,"[36] invoking Lao-tse and Jesus to define the "creative ideal ... [that] will make all form and function one . . . forms becoming more naturally significant of ideal and purpose, ultimate in economy and strength."[37] These forms manifest the essential architectural reality of interior space; the nature of that space is primarily "shelter that should be the essential look of any building,"[38] and it flows from the site:

The *room* must be seen as architecture, or we have no architecture . . . it is in the nature of an organic building to grow from its site, come out of the ground into the light—the ground itself held always as a component basic part of the building itself. And then we have primarily the new ideal of building as organic. A building dignified as a tree in the midst of nature.[39]

The familiar silhouette of the prairie houses is "natural" in Wright's sense in its radical asymmetry and outward-pushing spaces. Wright conceived of it as metaphysically unified like a body and not as a synthesis of distinguishable components; hence the notoriously uncomfortable furniture he designed for the interiors and his invective against ornament:

Have no posts, no columns, no pilasters, cornices or moldings or ornament; no divisions of the sort nor allow any fixtures whatever to enter as something added to the structure. Any building should be complete, including all within itself. Instead of many things, *one* thing.[40]

That "*one* thing" must be ornamented integrally, with "*structure-pattern made visibly articulate* and seen in the building as it is seen articulate in the structure of the trees or a lily of the fields."[41] This is "essential architecture," so Thoreauvian in spirit as to raise the question again of moral content determining a building's form; the evidence of Wright's many and various projects suggests, however, that the rhetoric works from a direction opposite that of Thoreau, with the architect imposing beautiful living upon the customer.

In the 1920s Le Corbusier, striving for a universal language of forms, began with the second of Greenough's organic phenomena, the machine; it is the engineer, he writes in *Vers une architecture*, who puts man in accord with universal law; it is the beauties of geometry that are most "natural." The axis of man's being, of nature, and of the universe is the consistency and unity of the organization of all phenomena, which are described by mathematics and physics and manifested in forms:

Geometry is the means, created by ourselves, whereby we perceive the external world and express the world within us. Geometry is the foundation. It is also the material basis on which we build those symbols which represent to us perfection and the divine.[42]

These forms are a natural language, from which we derive not a style but architecture beyond style.

54

The center of town, one of Le Corbusier's
seductive drawings, at once buoyant and
monumental, for the project *Une ville
contemporaine*, 1922.

Le Corbusier's projects of the early 1920s and his notorious *Plan Voisin* for Paris (1925) anticipate the systematization of his schemes of giant blocks in open green spaces in the *ville radieuse* project of the 1930s. The Paris project would have required the demolition of a substantial section of the Right Bank, but the advantages, Le Corbusier argued, were enormous: light and air, transformation of acres of stone and concrete into parks; in short, the reintroduction of nature into the city. The *ville radieuse* project reveals also Le Corbusier's enthusiasm for physical fitness; sports facilities are highlighted in the plan.

But the governing metaphors are not physical but metaphysical. Like Antonio Sant' Elia and Auguste Perret (his acknowledged master) before him, Le Corbusier envisioned more than a garden-city, more than a merely humane and efficient environment. The ruthlessness of the *Plan Voisin* implies a vision of an ultimate architecture of ideal forms, a solution to all the problems of the site, and consequently ahistorical and eternal. The ecstatic quality of the twenties projects in particular derives from the architect's submission to the aesthetic of the machine; their visual rhetoric of purity, brilliance, gigantism and replication bears out the language of "implacable" and "infallible" forms,[43] lifting a utopian project into a metaphor for Paradise. Informing every dimension of an ideal town, engineering manifests itself in symbolic rather than in primarily functional phenomena and particularly in rectangular solids and luminous planes of concrete or glass. Like the "bright surface" of Milton's heaven (*Paradise Lost*, VI, 472), Le Corbusier's glittering facades are characteristic of "a world without sin . . . 'bright surfaces' reflect the essences of archetypal beings; they are sharp, simple, unmistakable, instantly visible."[44] It is not merely coincidence that Le Corbusier's perspective drawings resemble the sets of an Inigo Jones masque; both are visual affirmations of an ideal order inherent in permanent, symmetrical forms.

The atheist Corbusier saw in the rigorous impersonality of the

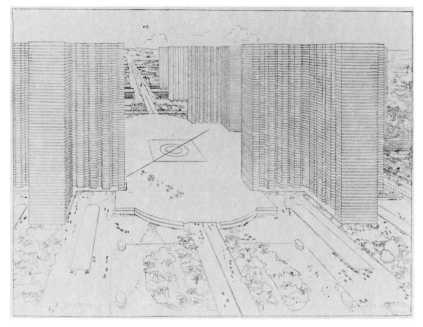

55 and 56

The Right Bank of Paris, as Le Corbusier
wished to reconstruct it, from the *Plan
Voisin* project, 1925. "There are fifty-four
cities in the island, all large and well built:
the manners, customs, and laws of which
are all the same, and they are all contrived
as near in the same manner as the ground
on which they stand will allow. . . . He that
knows one of their towns, knows them all"
(Sir Thomas More, *Utopia*, 1516, in the
first English translation by Ralph
Robinson, 1551).

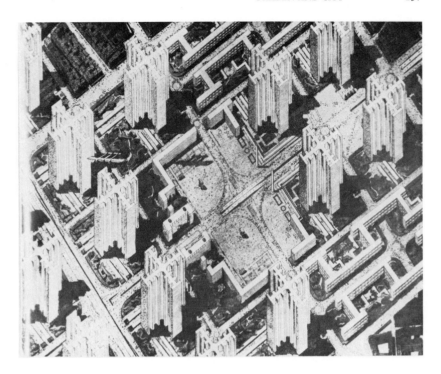

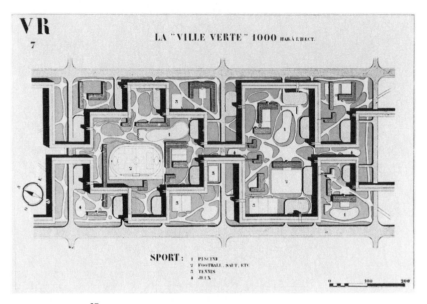

57

From Le Corbusier's *ville radieuse* project,
1930s.

machine the "evidence of a pure cosmic force uncontaminated by personal interference" and so sought to derive from it "a type of universal symbolism that would be transhistorical and non-conventional."[45] In this he resembles the architects of Chartres, the proportions of which cathedral, in Otto von Simson's eloquent testimony, "withdraw the structure from the realm of individual intention and render it anonymous, anonymous or impersonal like the great mathematical discoveries or the classical experiments of science."[46] Such architecture is "ontologically transparent,"[47] referring us immediately to the universals inhering in its forms, which is, of course, the ideal of the primitive hut in both its rationalistic and its anthropomorphic guise.

An anthropomorphic metaphor, in fact, governs the "radiant city." Its four functions, living, working, circulating, and recreating are understood biologically; the commercial center is the head, factories and warehouses the stomach, and so on. Wright similarly refers to the highways of Broadacre City as veins and arteries and to buildings as cellular tissue, and he promises that Broadacre City would "revive emasculated manhood."[48] Here there is no "style," only "Essential Style . . . naturally achieved from the nature of the building problem itself."[49] Both architects speak of liberation; for Le Corbusier the city-dweller is liberated into the natural advantages (space, air) of the country whereas Wright sees his plan as a liberation into the democracy that he termed "Usonian," founded on principles of the integrity of the family and the right to private space—an acre per individual. Here in the absence of "the *meum et tuum* of a profit system" (Wright's words), the first law of planning is the arcadian one of decentralization: "The true center (the only centralization allowable) in Usonian democracy, is the individual in his true Usonian family home."[50] His scheme too is eschatological beyond its humanism. In abolishing the city, he abolishes the country as well, by distributing the components of the city to the limits of the landscape, tying all together with arterial roads: "Such integrated distribution

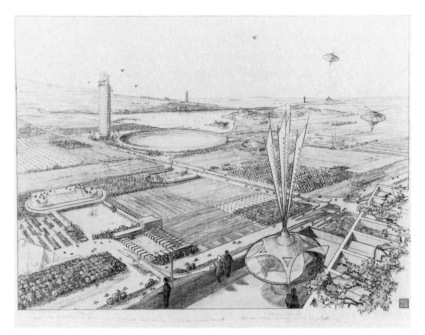

58 and 59

Romantic landscapes of an eternally
healthy, young America, from Frank Lloyd
Wright's Broadacre City project,
1934–1958: general view of a landscape;
and typical plan.

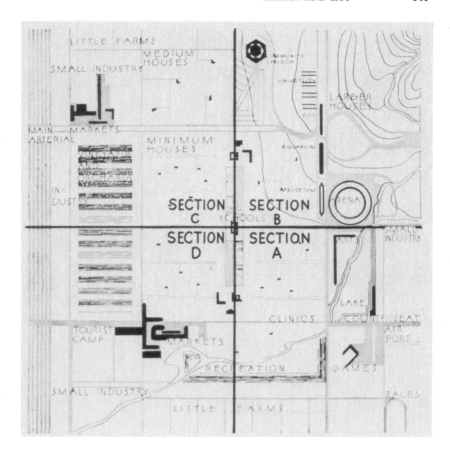

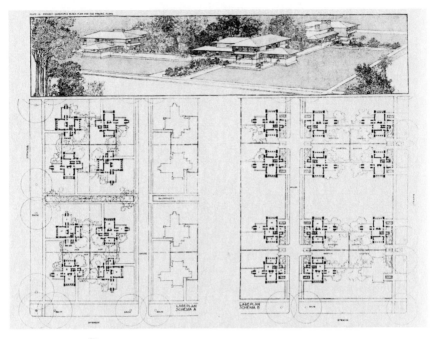

60

Arcadia shuns concentrations: Frank Lloyd
Wright's quadruple housing project, 1900,
an early example of Broadacre City
thinking; it recurs in *The Living City*, 1958.
Four houses divide a large suburban city
block at safe distances from one another,
but joined by a common wall enclosing
a central garden—the synthesis of
American privatism with communitarian,
egalitarian idealism.

of living, all related to ground—this composes the new city embracing this entire country, the Broadacre City of tomorrow. The
city becomes the nation."[51]

Wright's rhetoric as well as his projects are efforts to fulfill on a
vast and highly engineered scale the myth of the primitive hut; he is as
faithful as Le Corbusier to the belief in architecture's moral content
and as antagonistic as Le Corbusier not only to the Beaux-Arts school
but to time-bound forms generally. That Wright disliked much of
twentieth-century European architecture, including Le Corbusier's
projects, is of course another matter. But the obvious distinction
between their models of the ideal—that one proceeds from identification with organic, the other with geometric forms—points up their
connection along the axis of metaphor; each seeks a resolution of
antagonistic models of perfection, but from opposite poles. So with
Le Corbusier, centralized planning and replicated masses body forth
the mythos of the numinous palace, the temple, and the holy city
whereas the "grateful vicissitude"—to employ Raphael's characterization of the appearance of heaven (*Paradise Lost*, VI, 8)—of Wright's
asymmetrically evolving plans refers us to the pleasures of nature as
organized for our recreation and delight. Le Corbusier calls for right
architecture as an alternative to violent revolution;[52] Wright sees
right architecture at the basis of America's political survival.[53] Both
architects, "historicists" in Popper's sense, are children of the Enlightenment in demanding the implementation of universal laws or
in perceiving the arrival of the millennial age: "A higher *order* of the
spirit has dawned for modern life in this interior concept of lived-in
space playing with light, taking organic form as the reality of building
. . . people . . . now have a certain dignity and pride in their
environment; they see it has a meaning and a purpose. . . ."[54] Neither
the *ville radieuse* nor Broadacre City was more than a stage in a long
career, but both exemplified the working out on a huge scale of the
visionary rhetoric of modernism—that the new architecture

was to be authentic: That is, it was to be inevitable and predestined and in the nature of things. It was not to be one possibility among many, but the only possibility; and thus it was necessary that its determinants should seem to be outside the sphere of choice.[55]

Choice, however, is what both the aesthetics and the architectural politics of the last two decades have been all about—the famous "postmodernism" characterized by the rejection and even ridicule of the theory and much of the practice of the preceding hundred years.[56] Like Milton in the eyes of many critics of the thirties and forties, Wright and Le Corbusier, among other major figures, have been seen as destructive in influence; those who shuttle between bedroom suburb and office tower may be actors in a ghastly parody of their variously dispersed and concentrated systems of building. That the automobile is the serpent in Wright's spacious garden is too obvious to require comment although his rhapsodies on highways (*The Living City*, pp. 126–27) are still moving. At the opposite extreme, utopian urban programs continue to emerge, children of the "radiant city"; Brasília, the indirect product of a religious vision,[57] "unifying visual and social forces into one total, overpowering direction which allows no dissent, ambiguity, or memory,"[58] might be the New Jerusalem itself and has been challenged by the newer dogma that not the absence of convention but convention itself is a universality.[59] It is difficult to understand the 1970 project for a "No-Stop City: A Climatic Universal City" of the Studio Archizoom Associati (Florence) as other than an ironic comment upon the pretensions of those who would join city to countryside in an eschatological marriage. Both the idealist and the organicist subscribe to Alberti's unitary definition of the beautiful (quoted at the head of this chapter); both, through the elimination of superfluous or extraneous form, identify the achievement or perfection of architecture as the realization simultaneously of the beautiful and the necessary. Such a realization would amount to the invention of the "future," a metaphysical entity, which in Reinhold Niebuhr's sense is both inevitable and redemptive[60] and which has suffered an important symbolic defeat in the controversy, since 1968, over efforts to impose a grandiose *ville radieuse* master plan of concrete slabs and arterial roads on the hills surrounding Jerusalem.[61]

EPILOGUE

The state also of the blessed in Paradise, though never so perfect, is not therefore left without discipline, whose golden survaying reed marks out and measures every quarter and circuit of new Jerusalem.
(Milton, *The Reason of Church Government*, 1642)

The simile with which Andrew Marvell concludes "A Dialogue Between the Soul and Body," his terse and witty examination of man's unhappy union of flesh with spirit, goes beyond the imagery implied by the verb "to build" that precedes it. Here, in the concluding stanza of the dialogue, the Body retorts to the Soul:

> But Physick yet could never reach
> The Maladies Thou dost me teach;
> Whom first the Cramp of Hope does Tear:
> And then the Palsie Shakes of Fear.
> The Pestilence of Love does heat;
> Or Hatred's hidden Ulcer eat.
> Joy's chearful Madness does perplex:
> Or Sorrow's other Madness vex.
> Which Knowledge forces me to know;
> And Memory will not foregoe.
> What but a Soul could have the wit
> To build me up for Sin so fit?
> So Architects do square and hew,
> Green Trees that in the Forest grew.[62]

61

Lúcio Costa and Oscar Niemeyer, Brasília,
1956–1960: the mall.

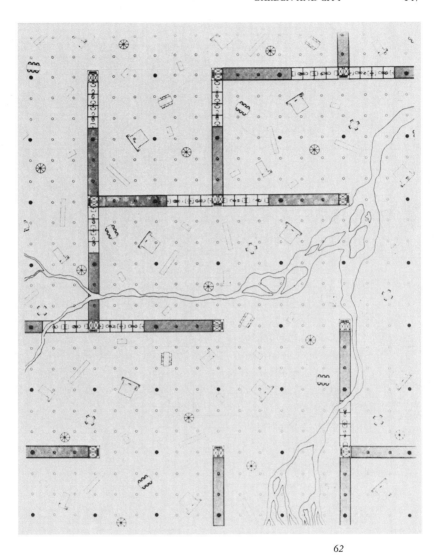

62

Studio Archizoom Associati, "No-Stop
City: A Climatic Universal City," 1970.

"Knowledge forces," and memory, mother of the muses and so the necessary condition for the existence of the arts, is a relentless discipliner of the body, thwarting its natural tendency to fall to a state of passionless rest. The arcadia of Marvell's "Body" is not so much destroyed as reorganized along lines both abstract and "unnatural," cutting across the grain of wood to conform to physically unimaginable requirements. Those requirements are of course metaphysical and are associated with the torment and death of the flesh, the "Forest," as well as with the art implicit in hewing and the formal idealities inherent in squaring. The Body has the last word, a poignant concession on the poet's part to a claim that has been superseded; knowledge and memory supersede innocence as the house supersedes the growing material of its construction. "For Sin so fit," the Body observes stingingly; it is left to Milton's God to justify the historical process that carries innocent flesh into time and consciousness, and builds Jerusalem on the wasteland that was Eden. Of course one may argue that nothing is really lost, that the larger design incorporates the earlier model. A wise prince in *The Winter's Tale*, defending the hybridization of flowers, calls up the orthodoxy that "over that art / Which . . . adds to nature, is an art / That nature makes," so including mental acts, and the manual acts that effect them, within the scope of "nature." But like Marvell's unconvinced Body, the girl to whom this argument is advanced is unimpressed. Architects pursuing respectively the visions of organic and ideal forms are the inheritors of these dialogues.

NOTES

Preface

1. Ellen Eve Frank, *Literary Architecture: Essays Toward a Tradition—Walter Pater, Gerard Manley Hopkins, Marcel Proust, Henry James* (Berkeley and Los Angeles: University of California Press, 1979), p. 96.

2. Norris Kelly Smith, *Frank Lloyd Wright: A Study in Architectural Content*, rev. ed. (Watkins Glen, N.Y.: American Life Foundation, 1979).

Introduction

1. Renato Poggioli, "The Oaten Flute," in his *The Oaten Flute: Essays on Pastoral Poetry and the Pastoral Ideal* (Cambridge, Mass.: Harvard University Press, 1975), pp. 1–2.

2. Stanley Stewart, *The Enclosed Garden* (Madison: University of Wisconsin Press, 1966); and Terry Comito, *The Idea of the Garden in the Renaissance* (New Brunswick, N.J.: Rutgers University Press, 1978).

3. "παράδεισος, 'ο, *an enclosed park* or *pleasure ground . . .* Zd. *pairidaeza* means *an enclosure*, and in Armen, *pardez* is *an enclosed garden*" (Henry George Liddell and Robert Scott, *Greek-English Lexicon*, 8th ed. [New York, 1897], p. 1127). "The word *pairidaeza* denotes a surrounding (*pairi* = Greek *peri*) wall made of a sticky mass (*daeza*) like clay (or dough)" (Leroy A. Campbell, *Mithraic Iconography and Ideology*, Etudes Préliminaires aux Religions Orientales dans l'Empire Romaine, 11 [Leiden: Brill, 1968], pp. 129–30).

4. Frank E. Manuel and Fritzie P. Manuel, *Utopian Thought in the Western World* (Cambridge, Mass.: Belknap Press of Harvard University Press, 1979), p. 38.

5. Philo Judaeus, *Questions and Answers on Genesis*, tr. Ralph Marcus, Loeb Classical Library (1953; rpt. Cambridge, Mass.: Harvard University Press, 1961), p. 4.

6. St. Gregory of Nyssa, cited in J. Daniélou, "Terre et paradis chez les pères de l'église," in *Eranos Jahrbuch, 22: Mensch und Erde* (Zurich: Rhein-Verlag, 1954), p. 434.

7. Honorius of Autun, *Elucidarium*, in J. P. Migne, ed., *Patrologiae Cursus Completus*, 221 vols. (Paris, 1844-1882), 172, col. 1117. Migne's edition is hereafter referred to as *Patrologia Latina*.

8. Citations of Milton's poetry throughout are taken from the edition of John Shawcross, *The Complete Poetry of John Milton*, rev. ed. (New York: Anchor, 1971).

9. John Bunyan, *The Holy City, or, the New Jerusalem*, in *The Complete Works of John Bunyan*, ed. Henry Stebbing, 4 vols. (New York: Johnson Reprint, 1970), I, 294; hereafter cited as Stebbing.

10. Colin Rowe and Fred Koetter, *Collage City* (Cambridge, Mass.: MIT Press, n.d.), p. 11.

ONE   EDEN AND JERUSALEM

1. Dolores Hayden, *Seven American Utopias: The Architecture of Communitarian Socialism, 1790-1975* (Cambridge, Mass.: MIT Press, 1976), p. 119. For information on the Nauvoo community, I am throughout indebted to this source, esp. to pp. 104-147.

2. Laurel B. Andrew, *The Early Temples of the Mormons: The Architecture of the Millennial Kingdom in the American West* (Albany: State University of New York Press, 1978), p. 12: "Temple ritual is a prerequisite for partaking of the joys of the afterlife, for it is only in a temple that certain necessary blessings can be received."

3. Thomas Hobbes, *Leviathan*, I, 13, in Nicolò Machiavelli, *The Prince*, tr. W. K. Marriott; and Thomas Hobbes, *Leviathan*, ed. Nelle Fuller, *Great Books of the Western World*, ed. Robert M. Hutchins et al., vol. 23 (Chicago: Encyclopedia Britannica, Inc., 1952), p. 85. Cf. Philo Judaeus, *De Opificio Mundi*, IV, 17–19, in *Philo*, tr. F. H. Colson and G. H. Whitaker, Loeb Classical Library, 12 vols. (Cambridge, Mass.: Harvard University Press, 1929; rpt. 1971), I, 14–19, who compares God to the architect of a city (*megalopolis*).

4. All Biblical quotations are from the Authorized or King James Version.

5. See Harry Caplan, "The Four Senses of Scriptural Interpretation and the Medieval Theory of Preaching," *Speculum*, 4 (1929): 282–90; and Walter J. Burghardt, "On Early Christian Exegesis," *Theological Studies*, 11 (1950): 78–116. Cf. William G. Madsden, "Earth the Shadow of Heaven: Typological Symbolism in Paradise Lost," *PMLA*, 75 (1960): 519–26; rpt. in his *From Shadowy Types to Truth: Studies in Milton's Symbolism* (New Haven: Yale University Press, 1968), pp. 87–113; and Barbara Nolan, *The Gothic Visionary Perspective* (Princeton: Princeton University Press, 1977), pp. 37, 44–45.

6. Marcel Proust, *A la recherche du temps perdu*, 3 vols. (Paris: Nouvelle Revue Française, 1954), I, 427.

7. *Institutio Oratoria of Quintilian*, tr. H. E. Butler, Loeb Classical Library, 4 vols. (Cambridge, Mass.: Harvard University Press, 1921–1922; rpt. 1958–1961), IV, 223.

8. Virgil, *Aeneid* VI, 673.

9. The formula is from Northrop Frye, *The Return of Eden* (Toronto: University of Toronto Press, 1965), p. 31.

10. Gaston Bachelard, *The Poetics of Space*, tr. Maria Jolas (Boston: Beacon Press, 1969), p. 185.

11. Virgil, *Aeneid* I, 314; see William Nelson, *The Poetry of Edmund Spenser* (New York: Columbia University Press, 1963), p. 159.

12. Bachelard, *Poetics of Space*, pp. 31–32, 47–48.

13. John Ruskin, *The Seven Lamps of Architecture* (London: Everyman's Library, 1969), p. 182.

14. Ulrich Simon, *Heaven in the Christian Tradition* (New York: Harper & Bros., 1958), pp. 44–45 and *passim*, records various uses of the term *paradise* signifying Eden either on earth or elsewhere in the Old Testament and in apocalyptic writings; see also Sister Mary Irma Corcoran, *Milton's Paradise with Reference to the Hexameral Background* (Washington, D.C.: Catholic University of America Press, 1945), pp. 17ff. and *passim*.

15. Frank E. Manuel and Fritzie P. Manuel, *Utopian Thought in the Western World* (Cambridge, Mass.: Belknap Press of Harvard University Press, 1979), pp. 38–40.

16. Ibid., p. 41.

17. Ibid., p. 42.

18. *Encyclopedia Judaica*, 16 vols. (Jerusalem: Keter Publishing House, 1971–1972), VII, 327.

19. Howard Rollin Patch, *The Other World According to Descriptions in Medieval Literature* (Cambridge, Mass.: Harvard University Press, 1950), p. 13.

20. Daniélou, "Terre et paradis," p. 448.

21. See Charles J. Sanford, *The Quest for Paradise* (Urbana: University of Illinois Press, 1961), p. 8; Manuel and Manuel, *Utopian Thought*, pp. 54ff.

22. The idea of a garden of Eden in the "third heaven" probably passed to St. Paul and St. Augustine from the first century A.D. Secrets of Enoch; see *The Apocrypha and Pseudepigrapha of the Old Testament in English*, ed. R. H. Charles, 2 vols. (1913; rpt. Oxford: Clarendon Press, 1968), II, 425, 429.

Citations of apocryphal and pseudepigraphic texts are from this edition and are cited hereafter as Charles, ed., *Apocrypha*.

23. *Theological Dictionary of the New Testament*, ed. Gerhard Friedrich, V, tr. and ed. Geoffrey W. Bromley (Grand Rapids, Mich.: Eerdmans, 1968), s.v. παράδεισος.

24. Stebbing, I, 333.

25. The full study of the garden of Canticles is Stewart's *Enclosed Garden*. The tradition of a fountain in Eden is examined by Paul A. Underwood, "The Fountain of Life in Manuscripts of the Gospels," *Dumbarton Oaks Papers*, 5 (1950; rpt. New York: Johnson Reprint, 1967), pp. 41–138.

26. Richard Rowlands, *Epithetes of Our Blessed Lady* (1601), cited in Stewart, *Enclosed Garden*, p. 42.

27. Robert Venturi, *Complexity and Contradiction in Architecture*, Museum of Modern Art Papers on Architecture, 2nd ed. (New York: Museum of Modern Art, 1977), p. 86.

28. Stewart, *Enclosed Garden*, p. 59.

29. See Claude J. Summers and Ted-Larry Pebworth, "Vaughan's Temple in Nature and the Context of 'Regeneration,'" *Journal of English and Germanic Philology*, 74, no. 3 (July 1975): 351–60.

30. U. Milo Kaufmann, *Paradise in the Age of Milton*, English Literary Studies, 11 (Victoria, B.C.: University of Victoria, 1978), pp. 7, 15–16.

31. I differ principally with Terry Comito, who equates the claustral garden with Eden in "Sacred Space and the Image of Paradise: The Cloister Garden," the second chapter of his *Idea of the Garden*.

32. Nolan, *Gothic Visionary Perspective*, p. 28.

33. Mircea Eliade, "The Yearning for Paradise in Primitive Tradition," *Daedalus*, 88, no. 2 (Spring 1959): 260; and Mircea Eliade, *The Myth of the Eternal Return*, Bollingen Series, 46 (Princeton: Princeton University Press, 1971), p. 12.

34. "Temples," *Encyclopedia of Religion and Ethics*, ed. James Hastings, 13 vols. (New York: Scribner's, n.d.), XII, 236–46.

35. Raphael Patai, *Man and Temple in Ancient Jewish Myth and Ritual* (London: Thomas Nelson, 1947), p. 131.

36. Eliade, *Myth of the Eternal Return*, p. 14.

37. Paul Piehler, *The Visionary Landscape: A Study in Medieval Allegory* (Montreal: McGill-Queen's University Press, 1971), p. 2.

38. Cf. Arabic name for Jerusalem, *El Quds* ("The Holy").

39. André Parrot, *The Temple of Jerusalem*, tr. B. E. Hooke, Studies in Biblical Archaeology, 5 (London: SCM Press, 1957), p. 51; see also G. Ernest Wright, "Solomon's Temple Resurrected," *Biblical Archaeologist*, 4, no. 2 (May 1941): 20.

40. Patai, *Man and Temple*, pp. 121–22.

41. *Midrash Tanhuma*, in ibid., p. 116.

42. Patai, *Man and Temple*, p. 90: "Solomon 'planted' trees of gold in the Temple and these brought forth fruit which served as nourishment for the priests." "Vegetable gold" is Milton's term for the fruit of the tree of life in *Paradise Lost*, IV, 220.

43. See Priscilla Soucek, "The Temple of Solomon in Islamic Legend and Art," in *The Temple of Solomon: Archaeological Fact and Medieval Tradition in Christian, Islamic, and Jewish Art*, ed. Joseph Gutmann, American Academy of

Religion: Society of Biblical Literature, Religion, and the Arts, 3 (Missoula, Mont.: Scholars Press, 1976), pp. 73–123.

44. Josephus, *Antiquitates Judaicae*, cited in Parrot, *Temple of Jerusalem*, p. 52.

45. Joseph Mede, *Clavis Apocalyptica ex innatis et insitis visionum characteribus eruta et demonstrata*, 2nd ed. (Cambridge, 1632).

46. Daniélou, "Terre et paradis," p. 454.

47. Simon, *Heaven in the Christian Tradition*, p. 84.

48. Cf. Wisdom of Solomon 9:8 (ca. 100 B.C.): "Thou gavest command to build a sanctuary in thy holy mountain, And an altar in the city of thy habitation, A copy of the holy tabernacle which thou preparedest from the beginning" (Charles, ed., *Apocrypha*, I, 549).

49. Ezra 3: 12–13 records the reactions.

50. See Joseph Gutmann, "When the Kingdom Comes: Messianic Themes in Medieval Jewish Art," *Art Journal*, 27, no. 2 (Winter 1967–1968): 172.

51. 1 Enoch 90:28–29: "And I stood up to see till they folded up that old house; and carried off all the pillars, and all the beams and ornaments of the house were at the same time folded up with it, and they carried it off and laid it in a place south of the land. And I saw till the Lord of the sheep brought a new house greater and loftier than that first, and set it up in the place of first which had been folded up: all its pillars were new, and its ornaments were new and larger than those of the first, the old one which he had taken away, and all the sheep within it" (Charles, ed., *Apocrypha*, II, 259).

52. Tobit 13:7–18, of disputed date; but see Charles, ed., *Apocrypha*, I, 174ff.

53. But cf. Sibylline Oracles, V, 418–27, of uncertain date but probably second century A.D., where a glorious Temple and city are restored in Israel; see Charles, ed. *Apocrypha*, II, 405.

54. See Simon, *Heaven in the Christian Tradition*, p. 47, for the continuation of Zionist belief in the restoration of the Temple or disbelief in its destruction; see also Nahum N. Glatzer, "Zion in Medieval Literature Prose Works," in his *Essays in Jewish Thought*, Judaic Studies Series, 8 (University: University of Alabama Press, 1978), pp. 135–48.

55. The episode of the cleansing of the temple, recorded in all four Gospels, "shows that the Temple is the accepted House of God and any practice which sullied its unique status as such was a matter for the deepest concern" (S. G. F. Brandon, *The Fall of Jerusalem and the Christian Church* [London: Society for Promoting Christian Knowledge, 1951], p. 37).

56. John Milton, *Means to Remove Hirelings* (1659).

57. Stebbing, I, 286.

58. *The Pearl*, tr. Sister Mary Vincent Hillman (Notre Dame, Ind.: University of Notre Dame Press, 1967); subsequent quotations are from this edition unless otherwise noted.

59. See Patricia M. Kean, *The Pearl: An Interpretation* (New York: Barnes & Noble, 1967), p. 211. Austin Farrar examines the allegorical significance of the city's components in *A Rebirth of Images: The Making of St. John's Apocalypse* (Westminster: Dacre Press, 1947) and *The Revelation of St. John the Divine* (Oxford: Clarendon Press, 1964); see also Milton R. Stern, "An Approach to *The Pearl*," *Journal of English and Germanic Philology*, 54 (1955): 691–92.

60. See R. H. Charles, *The Book of Enoch* (Oxford, 1893), pp. 80–81.

61. Line 29 is a crux. An alternative reading of *fede* as "fed" rather than

"faded" yields this situation: that the dreamer would exempt the lost pearl from physical decay and consequent use as nourishment for flowers while imagining it as already crowned with flowers present as tributes to its beauty. See Edward Vasta, "*Pearl*: Immortal Flowers and the Pearl's Decay," *Journal of English and Germanic Philology*, 66 (1967): 519-31.

62. Marie Borroff, *Pearl: A New Verse Translation* (New York: Norton, 1977), p. 24.

63. For a brief discussion, see A. C. Spearing, *The Gawain-Poet: A Critical Study* (Cambridge: Cambridge University Press, 1970), pp. 169-70.

64. John Ruskin, "Of Medieval Landscape," in his *Modern Painters*, 4th ed., 5 vols. (Boston, 1873), III, 274 (Part IV, ch. 14).

65. Ibid.

66. Derek Pearsall and Elizabeth Salter, *Landscapes and Seasons of the Medieval World* (Toronto: University of Toronto Press, 1973), p. 106.

67. Cf. ibid., p. 104: "[The dreamer] has exchanged a garden for a vision of the Earthly Paradise as a city or castle in a landscape—a familiar medieval variation upon the walled garden of Genesis. . . ."

68. See J. M. Evans, *Paradise Lost and the Genesis Tradition* (Oxford: Clarendon Press, 1968), esp. ch. 14; and Joseph E. Duncan, *Milton's Earthly Paradise* (Minneapolis: University of Minnesota Press, 1972), pp. 25, 38-39, 40.

69. *Patrologia Latina*, 82, col. 496.

70. For literary paradises and otherworldly places and structures generally, see Patch, *Other World*, esp. chs. 5-8; Sanford, *Quest for Paradise, passim*; and A. Bartlett Giamatti, *The Earthly Paradise and the Renaissance Epic* (Princeton: Princeton University Press, 1966).

71. Lorenzo de' Medici, tr. A. R. Turner, cited in Pearsall and Salter, *Landscapes and Seasons*, p. 80.

72. The pedigree of Claudian's Venusberg is somewhat obscure, but it includes Ovid's *Regia Solis* (*Metamorphoses* II) and the jeweled city amidst the Elysian Fields in Lucian's *True History*, Book II.

73. Alexander the Great comes upon Paradise, a walled city in India; see M[ary] Lascelles, "Alexander and the Earthly Paradise in Mediaeval English Writings," *Medium Aevum*, 5 (1936): 31–47, 79–104, 173–88.

74. George Kateb, *Utopia and Its Enemies* (New York: Schocken Books, 1972), p. 10.

75. Stebbing, I, 309, 312.

76. Harry Levin, "Paradise in Heaven and on Earth," *Encounter*, 32, no. 6 (June 1969): 35.

77. Michel Ragon, *Où vivrons-nous demain?* (Paris: Robert Laffont, 1963), p. 50: "la ville se ramassera sur elle-même, formera un tout, un bloc, qu'elle sera en soi architecture" ("the city will close in upon itself, will form an entity, a mass, so that it will be in and of itself architecture").

78. Ibid., p. 122, quoting the architect Edouard Albert: "It is the buoyant engineering of contemporary structural frameworks that inverts architectonic expression by incorporating in it the silence and transparency of the heavens."

Two   Poet and Architect

1. Relevant texts and a polemical critique of the gap between classical theory and practice in the "fine arts" are brought together by Frank P. Chambers, *Cycles of Taste: An Unacknowledged Problem in Ancient Art and Criticism* (Cambridge, Mass.: Harvard University Press, 1928).

2. S. H. Butcher, *Aristotle's Theory of Poetry and Fine Art*, 4th ed. (London: Macmillan, 1927), pp. 148–49.

3. Victor Mortet and Paul Deschamps, eds., *Recueil de textes relatifs à l'histoire de l'architecture et à la condition des architectes en France, au moyen âge: XIIe–XIIIe siècles*, 2 vols. (Paris: Picard, 1929), II, 21–23.

4. See St. Augustine: *De Musica*, VI, 57; *De Civitate Dei*, XXII, 24, 2; *De Libero Arbitrio*, II, 42; *De Ordine*, XIV; and *De Vera Religione*, XXX. The application of St. Augustine's aesthetics to architecture is examined in Otto von Simson, *The Gothic Cathedral: Origins of Gothic Architecture and the Medieval Concept of Order*, Bollingen Series, 48, 2nd ed. (1962; rpt. New York: Pantheon, 1965), pp. 23–26.

5. The terms *hard* and *soft* for versions of the ideal first state of man were coined by Arthur Lovejoy and George Boas, *A Documentary History of Primitivism and Related Ideas in Classical Antiquity* (Baltimore: Johns Hopkins University Press, 1935), pp. 9ff.

6. See esp. Harry Levin, *The Myth of the Golden Age in the Renaissance* (Bloomington: Indiana University Press, 1969).

7. Virgil, *Georgics*, Book II, esp. lines 458ff.; and Horace, *Epode* 2 and *Satires*, Book II, 6.

8. James A. Freeman, "The Roof Was Fretted Gold," *Comparative Literature*, 27 (1975): 254–66, skillfully traces the development of this rhetorical trope. I am indebted to this source for the following paragraph.

9. See, e.g., Horace's *Odes*, Book II, 15; and John Sekora, *Luxury: The Concept in Western Thought, Eden to Smollett* (Baltimore: Johns Hopkins University Press, 1977).

10. Andrew Marvell, "Upon Appleton House," line 216, in *The Poems and Letters of Andrew Marvell*, ed. H. M. Margoliouth, 3rd ed., rev. Pierre

Legouis and E. E. Duncan-Jones, 2 vols. (Oxford: Clarendon Press, 1971), I, 69; subsequent citations from Marvell's poems are from this edition.

11. Richard Crashaw, "Description of a Religious House," in *The Poems of Richard Crashaw*, ed. L. C. Martin, 2nd ed. (Oxford: Clarendon Press, 1957), p. 338.

12. See *The Iliad of Homer*, tr. Alexander Pope, ed. Maynard Mack et al., 2 vols. (London: Methuen, 1967), I, lxxvii; and *The Odyssey of Homer*, tr. Alexander Pope, ed. Maynard Mack et al., 2 vols. (London: Methuen, 1967), I, 241n.

13. Frank Lloyd Wright, *The Natural House* (New York: Horizon Press, 1954), p. 130.

14. *Seneca ad Lucilium Epistulae Morales*, tr. Richard M. Gummere, Loeb Classical Library, 3 vols. (Cambridge, Mass.: Harvard University Press, 1920; rpt. 1962), II, 410.

15. Seneca, *De Ira* III, 35, 5, in *Seneca: Moral Essays*, tr. John W. Basore, Loeb Classical Library, 3 vols. (1928; rpt. Cambridge, Mass.: Harvard University Press, 1958), I, 339.

16. Hugue de Fouilloi, *De Claustro Animae*, I, i, in Mortet and Deschamps, *Recueil de textes*, p. 92.

17. Mortet and Deschamps, *Recueil de textes*, pp. 23–24.

18. Joseph E. Duncan, *Milton's Earthly Paradise* (Minneapolis: University of Minnesota Press, 1972), p. 49.

19. Sekora, *Luxury*, p. 23.

20. Cicero: *Pro Sexto Roscio Amerino*, 46; *De Officiis*, I, 1; and *Ad Quintum Fratrem*.

21. Statius, *Silvae*, I, 3; II, 2; and Pliny, *Letters*, II, 17; V, 6.

22. Martial, *Epigrams*, Book III, 58 ("*Baiana villa, Basse, nostri Faustini*"); *Epigrams*, Book VII, 56, and Book VIII, 39, are in praise of Domitian's palace of A.D. 92.

23. Anon., *The Temple of Solomon* (London, 1724), preface.

24. Cf. Helen Rosenau, *The Ideal City: Its Architectural Evolution* (New York: Harper & Row, 1972), p. 14: "ideal planning . . . cogently illustrates the growth of 'social interest,' as described by Alfred Adler. Furthermore, the mandala, the circular plan, is a basic psychological factor in the theory of C. G. Jung."

25. St. Augustine, *De Quantitate Animae*, cap. XVI; see Richard Krautheimer, "Introduction to an 'Iconography of Medieval Architecture,'" *Journal of the Warburg and Courtauld Institutes*, 5 (1942): 9.

26. Rudolf Arnheim, *The Dynamics of Architectural Form* (Berkeley and Los Angeles: University of California Press, 1977), pp. 81–87.

27. For a discussion of this aspect of ideal Renaissance architecture, see Colin Rowe, "The Architecture of Utopia," in his *The Mathematics of the Ideal Villa and Other Essays* (Cambridge, Mass.: MIT Press, 1976), pp. 205–23.

28. *Homer: The Odyssey*, tr. Robert Fitzgerald (Garden City, N.Y.: Doubleday, 1961), pp. 125–26; subsequent translations of the *Odyssey* are from this edition.

29. On the archaeological validity of the metallic sequence of the ages, see H. C. Baldry, "Who Invented the Golden Age?" *Classical Quarterly*, n.s., 2 (1952): 83–92; J. Gwyn Griffiths, "Archaeology and Hesiod's Five Ages," *Journal of the History of Ideas*, 17 (1956): 109–19; H. C. Baldry, "Hesiod's Five Ages," *Journal of the History of Ideas*, 17 (1956): 553–54; and J. Gwyn Griffiths, "Did Hesiod Invent the Golden Age?" *Journal of the History of Ideas*, 19 (1958): 91–93.

30. *Ovid: Metamorphoses*, tr. Frank J. Miller, 2nd ed., Loeb Classical Library, 2 vols. (1921; rpt. Cambridge, Mass.: Harvard University Press, 1971), I, 61.

31. Heorot as an image of Paradise or of an ideal state of being is examined briefly in Edward B. Irving, Jr., *A Reading of Beowulf* (New Haven: Yale University Press, 1968), pp. 88–91; and at length by Alvin A. Lee, *The Guest-Hall of Eden: Four Essays on the Design of Old English Poetry* (New Haven: Yale University Press, 1972), pp. 171–223. See also the Anglo-Saxon poems *Genesis A*, lines 86–95; and *Christ and Satan*, lines 29, 93.

32. *Beowulf*, lines 93–97a; text and translation from *Beowulf: Anglo-Saxon Text with Modern English Parallel*, tr. John Porter (1975; rpt. London: Pirate Press, 1977).

33. We need not infer Gothic vaults, despite the arguments of Roland M. Frye, *Milton's Imagery and the Visual Arts: Iconographic Tradition in the Epic Poems* (Princeton: Princeton University Press, 1978), pp. 134–35; and A[my] L[ee] T[urner], "Arts of Design, Milton and the," in *A Milton Encyclopedia*, ed. William B. Hunter et al., 8 vols. (Lewisburg, Pa.: Bucknell University Press, 1978), I, 90–102. See also William A. McClung, "The Architecture of Pandaemonium," *Milton Quarterly*, 15, no. 4 (December 1981):109–12.

34. In denying a sharp distinction between a pastoral heaven and an urban hell, I differ with John Knott, Jr., *Milton's Pastoral Vision* (Chicago: University of Chicago Press, 1971).

35. John Ruskin, *The Seven Lamps of Architecture* (London: Everyman's Library, 1969), p. 15.

36. John Lightfoot, *The Temple, especially as it stood in the dayes of our Saviour* (London, 1650), p. 3.

37. See Helen Rosenau, *Vision of the Temple: The Image of the Temple of Jerusalem in Judaism and Christianity* (London: Oresko, 1979), p. 19.

38. See *The Interpreter's Bible*, ed. George A. Buttrick et al., 12 vols. (New York: Abingdon-Cokesbury, 1952-1957), I, 313; VI, 302f.

39. See *The New Bible Dictionary*, ed. J. D. Douglas et al. (1962; rpt. Grand Rapids, Mich.: Eerdmans, 1967), pp. 1242-50; plate xiv.

40. Rudolf Wittkower, *Architectural Principles in the Age of Humanism* (New York: Norton, 1971), p. 27.

41. Simson, *Gothic Cathedral*, pp. 19-20.

42. Ibid., pp. 21-24.

43. Ibid., pp. 37-38.

44. Ibid., p. 26.

45. Ibid., p. 30.

46. Ibid., p. 11.

47. See Jacob Judah Leon, *A Relation of the most memorable thinges in the Tabernacle of Moses, and the Temple of Salomon, According to text of scripture* (Amsterdam, 1675), pp. 14-15.

48. Simson, *Gothic Cathedral*, p. 125.

49. Ibid., p. 128.

50. Richard Stapleford, "Constantinian Politics and the Atrium Church," in *Art and Architecture in the Service of Politics*, ed. Henry A. Millon and Linda Nochlin (Cambridge, Mass.: MIT Press, 1978), pp. 2-19.

51. Johan Chydenius, *The Typological Problem in Dante: A Study in the History of Medieval Ideas*, Commentationes Humanarum Litterarum, 25 (Helsingfors: Societas Scientiarum Fennica, 1958), p. 71.

52. Stephen G. Nichols, Jr., "Signs of Royal Beauty Bright: Word and Image in the Legend of Charlemagne," *Olifant*, 4, no. 1 (1976): 21–47. André Grabar has derived the Palatine and other Western princely chapels from an equivalent structure in Constantinople, the Virgin of the Lighthouse (Θεοτόκος τοῦ Φάρου), constructed before 768, and discusses the tradition that Palatine chapels derive ultimately from the tent carried by Constantine during his desert campaign against the Persians to shelter an altar; thereby, he reconstituted the tabernacle and identified himself with Moses. See André Grabar, *Martyrium: Recherches sur le culte des reliques et l'art chrétien antique*, Collège de France: Fondation Schlumberger pour les Etudes Byzantines, 2 vols. and plates (Paris: Collège de France, 1943-1946), I, 560, 565-70.

53. See Earl Rosenthal, "A Renaissance 'Copy' of the Holy Sepulchre," *Journal of the Society of Architectural Historians*, 17, no. 1 (March 1958): 2-11; and Richard Krautheimer, "Santo Stefano Rotondo in Rome and the Rotunda of the Holy Sepulchre in Jerusalem," *Studies in Early Christian, Medieval, and Renaissance Art* (New York: New York University Press, 1968), pp. 69-106.

54. E. Baldwin Smith, *Architectural Symbolism of Imperial Rome and the Middle Ages*, Princeton Monographs in Art and Archaeology, 30 (Princeton: Princeton University Press, 1956).

55. Simson, *Gothic Cathedral*, pp. 137-38.

56. See Norman Cohn, *The Pursuit of the Millennium*, 2nd ed. (New York: Harper & Row, 1961), pp. 44-45.

57. Chydenius, *Typological Problem*, pp. 83-86.

58. See Carroll William Westfall, *In This Most Perfect Paradise: Alberti, Nicholas V, and the Invention of Conscious Urban Planning, 1447-1455* (University Park, Pa.: Pennsylvania State University Press, 1974), esp. pp. 57ff., 154ff.

59. Manuel and Manuel, *Utopian Thought*, p. 155.

60. Robert Lee Wolff, "The Three Romes: The Migration of an Ideology and the Making of an Autocrat," *Daedalus*, 88, no. 2 (Spring 1959): 291–311.

61. Karl Lehmann, "The Dome of Heaven," *Art Bulletin*, 27 (1945): 1–27. See also Grabar, *Martyrium*, II, 110n.

62. Manuel and Manuel, *Utopian Thought*, p. 178.

63. William L. MacDonald, *The Architecture of the Roman Empire, I: An Introductory Study* (New Haven: Yale University Press, 1965), p. 18.

64. And arguably of his political program to orientalize the empire; see H[ans] P[eter] L'Orange, *Studies on the Iconography of Sacred Kingship in the Ancient World*, Instituttet for Sammenlignende Kulturforskning, Serie A: Forelesninger, 23 (Oslo: H. Aschehoug, 1953). For opposing views, see Axel Boethius, "Nero's Golden House," *Eranos*, 44 (1946): 442–59; J. Ward Perkins, "Nero's Golden House," *Antiquity*, 30 (1956): 209–19; and Mac-Donald, *Architecture of the Roman Empire*, pp. 42–43.

65. *Suetonius: History of Twelve Caesars, Translated into English by Philemon Holland, Anno 1606*, ed. Charles Whibley, 2 vols. (1899; rpt. New York: AMS Press, 1967), II, 125.

66. MacDonald, *Architecture of the Roman Empire*, pp. 42, 37.

67. Ibid., p. 115.

68. John D. Hoag, *Western Islamic Architecture* (New York: Braziller, 1963), pp. 28–29.

69. William L. MacDonald, "Design and Technology in Hagia Sophia," *Perspecta: Yale Architectural Journal*, 4 (1957): 23.

70. See Gerhart B. Ladner, *The Idea of Reform: Its Impact on Christian Thought and Action in the Age of the Fathers* (Cambridge, Mass.: Harvard University Press, 1959), pp. 119–23; and Ernst Kantorowicz, *The King's Two*

Bodies: A Study in Medieval Political Theology (Princeton: Princeton University Press, 1957), ch. 8 and *passim*.

71. George Scheja, "Hagia Sophia und Templum Salomonis," *Istanbuler Mitteilungen*, 12 (1962): 49.

72. Richard Krautheimer, *Early Christian and Byzantine Architecture*, Pelican History of Art (1965; rpt. Baltimore: Penguin, 1967), pp. 160–61.

73. Frederick P. Bargebuhr, "The Alhambra Palace of the Eleventh Century," *Journal of the Warburg and Courtauld Institutes*, 19 (1956): 227–31.

74. Wittkower, *Architectural Principles*, p. 29n.

75. Leon Battista Alberti, in his *De Re Aedificatoria* (ca. 1450; pub. 1485), cites the circle and its derivatives (square, hexagon, octagon, decagon, dodecagon, the square plus one-half, the square plus one-third, and the square doubled) as the nine basic or perfect forms; see Wittkower, *Architectural Principles*, p. 3.

76. See Heinrich Wölfflin, *The Sense of Form in Art: A Comparative Psychological Study*, tr. Alice Muehsam and Norma Shatan (New York: Chelsea, 1958), *passim*, for the regularization of two-dimensional relationships in Renaissance Italy.

77. Jerónimo Prado and Juan Bautista Villalpando: Vol. I (Rome, 1596): *In Ezechielem Explanationes et Apparatus Urbis ac Templi Hierosolymitani*; Vol. II (Rome, 1604): *De Postrema Ezechielis Prophetae Visione* (with plates); Vol. III (Rome, 1604): *Apparatus Urbis ac Templi Hierosolymitani*.

78. Joseph Rykwert, *On Adam's House in Paradise: The Idea of the Primitive Hut in Architectural History*, Museum of Modern Art Papers on Architecture (New York: Museum of Modern Art, 1972), pp. 121–23; and René Taylor, "Architecture and Magic: Considerations on the *Idea* of the Escorial," *Essays in the History of Architecture Presented to Rudolf Wittkower*, ed. Douglas Fraser,

Howard Hibbard, and Milton J. Lewine (1967; rpt. London: Phaidon, 1969), pp. 81–109, esp. p. 97.

79. See Rykwert, *On Adam's House*, pp. 122–23, 126.

80. René Taylor, "Hermetism and Mystical Architecture in the Society of Jesus," *Baroque Art: The Jesuit Contribution*, ed. Rudolf Wittkower and Irma B. Jaffe (New York: Fordham University Press, 1972), p. 75.

81. Wittkower, *Architectural Principles*, p. 121.

82. For details of the controversy, see Rykwert, *On Adam's House*, pp. 127–40; and Wolfgang Herrmann, "Unknown Designs for the 'Temple of Jerusalem' by Claude Perrault," *Essays in the History of Architecture Presented to Rudolf Wittkower*, pp. 144–46.

83. The architect of Bath followed Villalpando's theory, if not his practice; see John Wood [the Elder], *The Origin of Building, or The Plagiarism of the Heathen Detected* (1741); and Rudolf Wittkower, "Federico Zuccari and John Wood of Bath," *Journal of the Warburg and Courtauld Institutes*, 6 (1943): 220–22.

84. See Pierre de la Ruffinière du Prey, "Solomonic Symbolism in Borromini's Church of S. Ivo alla Sapienza," *Zeitschrift für Kunstgeschichte*, 31 (1968): 216–32.

85. See Frank E. Baron, "Vitruvius and the Liberal Art of Architecture," *Bucknell Review*, 11, no. 4 (December 1963): 99–107.

86. Filarete, *Trattato d'Architettura*, Book I, fol. 2v., cited in Manuel and Manuel, *Utopian Thought*, p. 164.

87. James J. Yoch, "Architecture as Virtue: The Luminous Palace from Homeric Dream to Stuart Propaganda," *Studies in Philology*, 75, no. 4 (Fall 1978): 410–12.

88. The definitive analysis of the politics of the Stuart court masque is Stephen Orgel's *The Illusion of Power: Political Theater in the English Renaissance* (Berkeley and Los Angeles: University of California Press, 1975).

89. See D. J. Gordon, "Poet and Architect: The Intellectual Setting of the Quarrel Between Ben Jonson and Inigo Jones," *Journal of the Warburg and Courtauld Institutes*, 12 (1949): 152–78.

THREE   GARDEN AND CITY

1. Roland Frye, *Milton's Imagery and the Visual Arts*, pp. 192–98, examines the iconographic tradition in Christian art before Milton's time.

2. J. C. Gray, "Emptiness and Fulfillment as Structural Pattern in *Paradise Lost*," *Dalhousie Review*, 53 (1973): 78–91.

3. I am indebted to the late Reuben Brower for pointing out this correspondence. Cf. James Turner, *The Politics of Landscape* (Cambridge, Mass.: Harvard University Press, 1979), pp. 28–29.

4. Marvell, "Upon Appleton House," lines 97–100.

5. Cf. John R. Knott, Jr., "Milton's Heaven," *PMLA*, 85 (1970): 489; Joseph E. Duncan, *Milton's Earthly Paradise* (Minneapolis: University of Minnesota Press, 1972), p. 238; and J. B. Broadbent, *Some Graver Subject: An Essay on Paradise Lost* (New York: Barnes & Noble, 1960), p. 171.

6. John M. Steadman, *Epic and Tragic Structure in Paradise Lost* (Chicago: University of Chicago Press, 1976), p. 26.

7. Duncan, *Milton's Earthly Paradise*, p. 238, is representative but, I think, misguiding in polarizing the three realms along axes of time/time-

lessness and nature/artifice: "Heaven is radiant with the glory of God, and Hell has artificial lighting . . . while Heaven is eternity and Hell is monotony, Paradise as the realm of nature is the realm of time, human history, and moral struggle." All three realms exist in an historical context: events unforeknown (except to God) take place in each, requiring appropriate responses and altering the perceived pattern of future time; angels celestial and infernal are summoned to council and confronted with options. Hell is not monotonous, at least not when we leave it in Book X, with Satan's reentry and the amazing sequence of events. The interior of Pandaemonium has artificial lights, but as heaven has gold pavements (I, 682), artifice alone is a weak disqualification; and the changing light of heaven, acknowledged to be superfluous to need but present for "change delectable" (V, 629), makes a weak contrast as well.

8. Knott, "Milton's Heaven," p. 489.

9. Michael Murrin, "The Language of Milton's Heaven," *Modern Philology*, 74, no. 4 (May 1977): 354; cf. Jackson I. Cope, "Time and Space as Miltonic Symbol," *ELH*, 26 (1959): 497–513; and Roy Daniells, *Milton, Mannerism, and Baroque* (Toronto: University of Toronto Press, 1963), pp. 88–89.

10. As H. F. Robins points out in "Satan's Journey: Direction in '*Paradise Lost*,'" *Journal of English and Germanic Philology*, 60 (1961): 699–711, Satan ought to have known the shape of his fatherland. But I cannot conclude with him that the indeterminacy merely refers us to Satan's distant point of observation. Memory ought to preempt a simply optical ambiguity. The question remains whether the shape is knowable at all, at least to the audience of the epic.

11. D. C. Allen, *The Harmonious Vision: Studies in Milton's Poetry* (Baltimore: Johns Hopkins University Press, 1954), p. 99: "the amarant . . . is not a real flower at all but an ideality inexpressible in terms of earthly flora."

12. Christopher Grose, *Milton's Epic Process: Paradise Lost and Its Miltonic Background* (New Haven: Yale University Press, 1973), p. 238.

13. Isabel G. MacCaffrey, *Paradise Lost as "Myth"* (Cambridge, Mass.: Harvard University Press, 1959), p. 161.

14. For the acanthus I am indebted to John Carey and Alastair Fowler, eds., *The Poems of John Milton* (London: Longmans, 1968), p. 653n.

15. Broadbent, *Some Graver Subject*, p. 181.

16. See Marcia R. Pointon, *Milton and English Art* (Toronto: University of Toronto Press, 1970), esp. plates 11, 19, 21, 33, 37, 48, 143, 156.

17. Philo Judaeus, *Questions and Answers on Genesis*, p. 15.

18. Cf. Franz Cumont, *After Life in Roman Paganism* (New Haven: Yale University Press, 1922), ch. 8.

19. Northrop Frye, *Fearful Symmetry: A Study of William Blake* (Princeton: Princeton University Press, 1947), p. 91; cf. pp. 127–28, 224, 230, 231, 237, 238, 363, 368.

20. Rykwert, *On Adam's House*, p. 13.

21. William Alexander McClung, *The Country House in English Renaissance Poetry* (Berkeley and Los Angeles: University of California Press, 1977).

22. Marvell, "Upon Appleton House," lines 9–16.

23. For a summary of the contributions of Roland Fréart, Claude Perrault, the abbé Cordemoy, and others, see John Summerson, *The Classical Language of Architecture* (Cambridge, Mass.: MIT Press, 1976), ch. 5; cf. Wolfgang Herrmann, *Laugier and Eighteenth-Century French Theory* (London: Zwemmer, 1962), pp. 46–52.

24. Jacques François Blondel restated the Vitruvian orthodoxy in the *Encyclopédie* of 1751: "L'architecture a commencé par les cabanes et a fini par les palais"; see Herrmann, *Laugier*, p. 47.

25. John Ruskin, *The Stones of Venice*, 4th ed., 3 vols. (Orpington, Kent, 1886), I, 23–25 (ch. 1, parts 36–39). Efforts after Laugier to define the "authentic" and original style of architecture are discussed in Rykwert, *On Adam's House*, chs. 3–4.

26. *Plutarch's Lives*, tr. Bernadotte Perrin, Loeb Classical Library, 11 vols. (Cambridge, Mass.: Harvard University Press, 1914; rpt. 1967), I, 243.

27. Sigfried Giedion, *Space, Time, and Architecture*, 5th ed. (Cambridge, Mass.: Harvard University Press, 1967), p. 291.

28. Horatio Greenough, "American Architecture" (1843), in *Form and Function: Remarks on Art, Design, and Architecture*, ed. Harold A. Small (Berkeley and Los Angeles: University of California Press, 1947; rpt. 1974), p. 86.

29. Henry David Thoreau, *Walden*, ed. J. Lyndon Shanley (Princeton: Princeton University Press, 1971), p. 47; subsequent citations are from this edition.

30. Cited in *The Literature of Architecture: The Evolution of Architectural Theory and Practice in Nineteenth-Century America*, ed. Don Gifford (New York: Dutton, 1966), p. 196.

31. Ibid., p. 197.

32. Karl Popper, *The Open Society and Its Enemies*, rev. ed. (Princeton: Princeton University Press, 1950), pp. 452–53.

33. David Watkin, *Morality and Architecture: The Development of a Theme in Architectural History and Theory from the Gothic Revival to the Modern Movement* (Oxford: Clarendon Press, 1977), p. 53.

34. Le Corbusier's "modulor" is well known; cf. Wright, *Natural House*, p. 17.

35. Greenough, "American Architecture," pp. 57–61.

36. Wright, *Natural House*, p. 22.

37. Ibid., p. 32.

38. Ibid., p. 16.

39. Ibid., pp. 49–50.

40. Ibid., p. 20.

41. Ibid., p. 65.

42. Le Corbusier, *The City of To-morrow* [*Urbanisme*], tr. Frederick Etchells (1929; rpt. London: Architectural Press, 1947), p. 13.

43. Le Corbusier, *Towards a New Architecture*, tr. Frederick Etchells (1960; rpt. New York: Praeger, 1972), p. 198.

44. MacCaffrey, *Paradise Lost as "Myth,"* p. 163.

45. Charles Jencks, *Le Corbusier and the Tragic View of Architecture* (Cambridge, Mass.: Harvard University Press, 1973), p. 54.

46. Simson, *Gothic Cathedral*, p. 230.

47. Ibid., p. 231.

48. Frank Lloyd Wright, *The Living City* (New York: New American Library, 1970), pp. 124, 98.

49. Ibid., p. 97.

50. Ibid., pp. 152, 231; cf. Wright, *Natural House*, p. 187.

51. Wright, *Living City*, p. 127.

52. Le Corbusier, *Towards a New Architecture*, pp. 249–69.

53. Wright, *Natural House*, p. 187.

54. Ibid., pp. 32, 135.

55. Colin Rowe, "Neo-'Classicism' and Modern Architecture I," in his *The Mathematics of the Ideal Villa and Other Essays* (Cambridge, Mass.: MIT Press, 1976), p. 125.

56. Representative critiques include Venturi, *Complexity and Contradiction in Architecture*; Charles Jencks, *The Language of Post-Modern Architecture*, rev. ed. (London: Academy Editions, 1977); Brent C. Brolin, *The Failure of Modern Architecture* (New York: Van Nostrand Reinhold, 1976); and Peter Blake, *Form Follows Fiasco: Why Modern Architecture Hasn't Worked* (Boston: Little, Brown, 1977). Cf. Lewis Mumford, *The Highway and the City* (New York: Harcourt, 1963), pp. 162–75.

57. The prophetic dream of St. Giovanni Bosco (1815–1888) of a great city of the blessed between the 15th and 20th parallels.

58. Charles Jencks, *Architecture 2000: Predictions and Methods* (New York: Praeger, 1971), p. 10.

59. Jencks, *Le Corbusier*, p. 54.

60. See Ernest L. Tuveson, *Millennium and Utopia: A Study in the Background of the Idea of Progress* (Berkeley and Los Angeles: University of California Press, 1949), p. ix.

61. For an analysis see Arthur Kutcher, *The New Jerusalem: Planning and Politics* (Cambridge, Mass.: MIT Press, 1975).

62. Andrew Marvell, "A Dialogue Between the Soul and Body," pp. 22–23.

ACKNOWLEDGMENTS FOR ILLUSTRATIONS

1. Musée Condé, Chantilly, ms. 65, fol. 25v. Photographie Giraudon, Paris.
2. By permission of the Houghton Library, Harvard University.
3. Gemäldegalerie der Akademie der bildenden Künste, Vienna.
4. Courtesy of the Edward E. Ayer Collection, Newberry Library, Chicago.
5. The Missouri Historical Society, St. Louis.
6. Bild-Archiv der Österreichischen Nationalbibliothek, Vienna, cod. 2554, fol. 1.
7. Bibliothèque Sainte-Geneviève, Paris, cod. 218, fol. 2r. Photographie Giraudon, Paris.
8. By permission of the Huntington Library, San Marino, California.
9. Reprinted from Walter Horn and Ernest Born, *The Plan of St. Gall: A Study of the Architecture & Economy of, & Life in a Paradigmatic Carolingian Monastery.* 3 vols. Berkeley: University of California Press, 1979. I, xxviii.
10. Collection Teddy Kollek, Jerusalem. Photograph, Israel Museum.
11. By permission of the Houghton Library, Harvard University. Photograph by Barry Donahue.
12. Alinari/Editorial Photocolor Archives. SEF/EPA, Inc.
14. Reproduced by permission of the Trustees of the Wallace Collection.
15. By permission of the Houghton Library, Harvard University.
17. The British Library, Harleian ms. 4425, fol. 12v.
18. By permission of the Houghton Library, Harvard University. Photograph by Barry Donahue.
19. By permission of the Houghton Library, Harvard University.
22 and 23. Reprinted from *The Mathematics of the Ideal Villa and Other Essays*, by Colin Rowe, by permission of the MIT Press, Cambridge, Massachusetts, Copyright © 1976 by the Massachusetts Institute of Technology.
24. Alinari/Editorial Photocolor Archives. SEF/EPA, Inc.
25. Courtesy of Harvard College Library.
26. Theodore Busink.
27. Collection Teddy Kollek, Jerusalem, Photograph, Israel Museum.

28. National Gallery of Art, Washington, D.C. Samuel H. Kress Collection.

29. By permission of the Houghton Library, Harvard University. Photograph by Barry Donahue.

30. Courtesy of Dumbarton Oaks Research Library and Collection, Washington, D.C.

31 and 32. Andover-Harvard Theological Library.

33 and 34. Courtesy of Harvard College Library.

35. J. S. Billings Memorial Collection, Arts, Prints, and Photographs Division, New York Public Library.

36. Andover-Harvard Theological Library.

37. Church Archives, Church of Jesus Christ of Latter-Day Saints.

38. Laurel B. Andrew.

40, 41, and 42. By permission of the Houghton Library, Harvard University.

43. Devonshire Collection, Chatsworth. Reproduced by permission of the Chatsworth Settlement Trust. Plate from *Inigo Jones*, by Stephen Orgel and Roy Strong. Reproduced with permission.

44. Alinari/Editorial Photocolor Archives. SEF/EPA, Inc.

45 and 46. Courtesy, Museum of Fine Arts, Boston.

47 and 48. By permission of the Houghton Library, Harvard University.

51 and 52. Courtesy of Harvard College Library. Photographs by Barry Donahue.

53. By permission of the Huntington Library, San Marino, California.

54, 55, and 56. Architectural Publishers Artemis, Zürich, Switzerland.

57. Editions Vincent Fréal et Cie, Paris.

58. Broadacre City view, Copyright © The Frank Lloyd Wright Foundation, 1958.

59. Broadacre City plan, Copyright © The Frank Lloyd Wright Foundation, 1957.

60. Ladies Home Journal Block plan, Copyright © The Frank Lloyd Wright Foundation, 1963.

61. Norma Evenson.

62. Studio Archizoom Associati, Florence, Italy.

INDEX

Aachen, as *Nova Roma*, 71, 72
Abelard, Peter, 69
Acts, 30
Adam (and Eve), 16, 19, 20, 44, 52,
 103, 107, 110
Adonis, garden of, 110
Aeneid, 49, 104
Agrippa, 77
Alberti, Leon Battista, 72, 82, 98,
 101, 144
Alcinous, palace of, 62, 98
Alexander VII, Pope, 92
Alexander legends, 41
Alhambra, 77, 79
Allen, D.C., 106
Ambrose, Saint, 50
Amos, 26
Andreas, 64
Anthemius of Tralles, 78
Appleton House, Yorkshire, 105,
 115
Aquinas, Saint Thomas, 92
Aratus, 48
Arcadia: Eden, 2
Architect: in epic poetry, 64; as
 uomo universale, 98
Architectural mysticism, 71
Architecture: relationship of craft
 to nature, 2; conceptions of, 7; of
 nature, 14; of heaven, 14, 15;

phenomena of, 15; and poetry,
 17; in antique aesthetic and phi-
 losophical systems, 47; linked
 with music, 48; as a mechanical
 art, 48; as a concept of behavior,
 48, 50; literary, 48–50; as a pattern of degeneration, 49; and
 morals, 49–51; as a metonym for
 craft, 50; anthropomorphism of,
 50, 126, 128, 129, 130, 139; organic, 50, 131, 132, 133, 143; iron
 age, 51; paradisal, 52; ideal, 52,
 53; celestial, 53; epic, 64; and
 music, 69; Christian, 70; conver-
 sion to religious use, 70, 71;
 Gothic, 70, 119; celestial symbolism, 74; dominance of ecclesiastic over civil, 74; equation
 of physical and moral beauty,
 74; space as the essence of, 75;
 Byzantine, 79; Renaissance, 82;
 shift to pre-salvationist, 82; of
 utopia, 92; imitative of nature,
 93; of Paradise, 106; bower, 109,
 110, 111, 114; of Eden, 110; in
 georgic literature, 114; in stoic
 thought, 114, 115, 123; primitive
 hut, 114, 118, 129; morality attributed to, 115, 116, 123; assimilation to nature, 118; neoclassicism, 118; functional, 118, 131;
 assimilation of nature to, 119;

Architecture (*continued*)
ethical validation of, 119; morality of form, 123; morality of function, 123, 126, 129; modern, 130, 143; as a moral act, 131; synthesis of arcadian and utopian, 131; modern theory, 131; mechanistic, 131, 132, 133, 135; of humanism, 132; luxury in, 132; of ideal forms, 135; as a metaphor for Paradise, 135; arcadian, 139; Usonian, 139; Beaux Arts School, 143; geometric, 143; deterministic, 144; postmodern, 144

Ariosto, Ludovico, 41
Aristides, 48
Aristotle, 16, 47, 48, 114
Arnheim, Rudolf, 61
Astraea, goddess of justice, 49
Atlantis, use of square and circle in, 61
Augustine, Saint, 15, 17, 18, 31, 39, 48, 61, 69
Automobile, effect of, 144
Averlino, Antonio. *See* Filarete

Babylon, as gate of gods, 25
Bachelard, Gaston, 16
Barbaro, Daniele, 98
Baruch (the prophet), 27
Beatrice, 38
Beauty, definition of, 101
Beowulf, 63
Bernard of Clairvaux, Saint, ⁵⌐
Blake, William, 110, 114
Book of Mormon, 92
Borromini, Francesco, 92
Bower, 16, 109, 110, 111, 114. *See also* Primitive hut
Brasília, 144

Broadacre City, 7, 131, 139, 143
Broadbent, J. B., 110
Bronze Age, 49
Bunyan, John, 19, 31, 45
Byzantine architecture, 79

Canticles, 19, 20, 41
Cathedral, Gothic, 82
Cathedral School of Chartres, 69
Celestial architecture, 53
Celestial city: palace in, 14; temple in, 14
Celestial kingdom, as city and state of being, 34
Celestial space on earth, properties of, 54, 74
Celestial symbolism, 74
Chapman, George, 93, 98
Charlemagne, 71
Chartres Cathedral, 139
Chasteau d'Amour, 40
Chloridia, 100
Chronicles, 68
Chrysogonos, 52
Chrysostom, Saint John, 51
Church of the Holy Sepulchre, 71
Cicero, 52
Circle: as symbol, 54; symbolism of, 61; use in Atlantis, 61
City: heavenly, 31; Italian Renaissance projection of, 74
City of God (Enoch), 19
City of God (St. Augustine), 17, 103
Claudian, 40, 62, 65, 101
Claudian version of Eden, 41
Clavis Apocalyptica, 26
Clement, Saint, 51
Cockaigne, land of, 41
Collage City, 7

Colonna, Francesco, 79
Comito, Terry, 3
Commedia, 31
Constantine, 79
Constantinople, imperial palace at, 79
Constituents of forms, 53
Construction, as a natural act, 98
Content, morality of, 130
Corbusier. *See* Le Corbusier
Corinthians, 30
Craft to nature, relationship of, 2
Crashaw, Richard, 50
Critias, 61
Crusade, First (1099), 72
Cube, as a symbol, 61
Cyprian, Saint, 50

Dante, Alighieri, 31, 35, 38
da Vinci. *See* Leonardo da Vinci
De Architectura, 93, 98, 118
De Consecratione, 70
De Re Aedificatoria, 98, 101
De Rerum Natura, 93
Dome: of the Rock, 26; importance of, 74, 77, 79; on a drum, 77; Neronian, 77; as the vault of heaven, 77, 79
Domitian, palace of, 52, 74

Eden: arcadian, 2, 14; vulnerability of, 3, 16; utopian vision of, 7; Smith's version of, 13; quest for, 14; utopian, 14; as a model for a state of bliss, 17; as the Paradise to come, 17; in space and time, 18; as a third heaven, 18; as a garden-city, 19; in New Jerusalem, 19; as water and tree of life, 19; walled, 20; as a fortress, 24; as a garden of delights, 39; survival

of, 39; as a walled garden, 39, 41; Claudian version of, 41; in *Paradise Lost*, 44; in pastoral and georgic literature, 44; synthesis of organic and inorganic, 107–111 *passim*; architecture of, 110; as a city, 114
Eden/Jerusalem dichotomy, 13
Elijah, 18
Elysian Fields, 16
Enoch: third heaven, 18; City of God, 19; Ethiopic Book of, 34
Ephesians, 30, 70
Ephraem, Syrus, 26
Epigrams, 115
Epithalamium (Claudian), 40, 62, 101
Epode 2 (Horace), 50
Erlach, Johann Fischer von, 83
Essai sur l'architecture, 118
Essay on Criticism, 82
Ethiopic Book of Enoch, 34
Eumaeus, farm of, 64
Eupalinos, or, The Architect, 47, 48
Eusebius, 78
Eustathius, 50
Exodus, 25, 27, 65
Ezekiel, 18, 19, 26, 39, 68, 83
Ezra, 17, 30

Faerie Queene, 7, 110
Fairfax, Baron, 115
Filarete, 61, 93, 98
Fitzgerald, Robert, 62
Form: constituents of, 53; morality of, 130; universal language of, 133
Fortunate Isles, 41
Fouilloi, Hugue de, 51
Fra Angelico, 101

Frye, Northrop, 114
Function, morality of, 129

Galatians, 30
Gate of gods, 25
Genesis, 3, 20, 104, 114
Genesis garden, 39
Geometry, 133
Georgic literature, 14
Giedion, Sigfried, 123, 131
Giorgio, Francesco di, 61
Gold, as a symbol, 45
Golden age, 14, 39, 45, 49
Golden house of Nero, 51, 75
Golgonooza, 114
Gondola, Andrea dalla. *See*
  Palladio
Gorgias, 48
Greenough, Horatio, 123, 126,
  130, 132, 133
Gregory of Nyssa, Saint, 3
Grendel, 63
Grosseteste, Robert, 40
Gudea of Lagash, 25

Hagia Sophia, 75, 78, 79
Hagia Soros, 71
Harmonious proportion, 70
Hawkins, Henry, 20
Heaven: architecture of, 14;
  walled, 65; as a walled city, 105,
  106, 109; synthesis of organic and
  inorganic, 106, 107, 109, 111;
  walls of, 109
Heaven and Hell, 63
Hebrews, 30
Hell, 65
Heorot, 63, 64
Hephaestus (*also* Vulcan), palace
  of, 62, 64

Herod, 68
Herodian, 72
Herodotus, 61
Hesiod, 48, 51
Hildebert of Lavardin, 30
Histories, 61, 72
Hoag, John, 77
Hobbes, Thomas, 14
Holland, Philemon, 75, 77
Holy Sepulchre, Church of Con-
  stantine, 71
Homer, 53, 64, 98
Honorius of Autun, *Elucidarium*, 3
Horace, 49, 50, 115
Houselessness, 16
Howard, Ebenezer, 130, 131
Hrothgar, palace of. *See* Heorot
Hugh of St. Victor, 48
Hugo, Emperor, palace of, 79
Huon de Bordeaux, 41
Huxley, Aldous, 63
Hyperboreans, land of, 41

Ideal architecture, 52, 53
Iliad, 62, 64
Inferno, 35
Iron age, 49, 51
Isaiah, 25, 27
Isidore of Seville, 39, 50
Isidorus of Miletus, 78
Italia liberata dai Goti, 98
Italian Renaissance, 74

Jehovah, 26, 65
Jerome, Saint, 50
Jerusalem: utopia, 2; Smith's ver-
  sion of, 13; as the holy city, 25;
  Jehovah's departure from, 26;
  sack of, 27; structure of, 34; in
  Pearl, 38; translation of heaven

to Apocalypse, 39; subversion of, 44; transfer of the Temple to, 71; First Crusade, 72; reestablishment of kingdom of, 72; Urban II's description of, 72; yield of historical role, 72; on the wasteland that was Eden, 148
Joachim of Fiore, 25
John of Patmos, 9, 19
Jones, Inigo, 93, 98, 100, 135
Jonson, Ben, 98, 100, 115, 116
Josephus, 26
Justin Martyr, 39
Juvenal, 50

Kaufmann, U. Milo, 24
Kings, 68, 69
Koetter, Fred, 7

Lamy, Bernard, 83
Last Judgment, painting by Fra Angelico, 101
Laugier, Marc-Antoine, 118, 119, 129, 130
Laws, 61
Le Clerc, Dom Jean, 70
Le Corbusier (pseud. of Charles-Édouard Jeanneret), 7, 131, 132, 133, 135, 143, 144
Lee, Alvin, 63
Lehmann, Karl, 74
Leonardo da Vinci, 98
Lethaby, William, 130
Levi, 18
Lightfoot, John, 68
Literalism, 82
Literature: georgic, survival of Eden in, 44; pastoral, survival of Eden in, 44; arcadian, 48; georgic, 48

Living City, The, 144
Lorini, Buonaiuto, 61
l'Orme, Philibert de, 83
Lucretius, 93
Luke, 18, 19
Luxury: definition of, 52; rehabilitation of, 119; in architecture, 132
Lycurgus, 123

McCaffrey, Isabel, 109
McDonald, William, 77
Maimonides, 27
Maison Carrée, 118
Marco Polo, on paradise, 41
Mark, 30
Martial, 50, 52, 74, 115
Martin, Jan, 93
Marvell, Andrew, 24, 49, 105, 116, 145, 148
Mass and luminosity, 62, 63, 65, 68, 70
Matthew, 30
Mede, Joseph, 26
Medici, Lorenze de', 40
Medieval economics, 51
Menelaus, palace of, 62, 63
Messiah, 18
Metamorphoses, 49, 62
Michael, Archangel, 104
Midrash Konen, 18
Milton, John, 65, 92, 101, 103, 104, 105, 106, 109, 111, 114, 135, 144, 145, 148
Mining, taboos, 64
Modern architecture, ecstatic component of, 7
Moral Epistle 90, 45, 47, 51, 129
Mormon community of Nauvoo, Illinois, 9

Moscow, as third Rome, 74
Moses, 25, 27
Mount Moriah, 27
Muhammad V, 78
Mulciber, 64, 105
Murrin, Michael, 106, 107
Musaeus, 93
Music and architecture, 69
Mysticism, 71

Natural artifacts, 116
Nature, architecture of, 14
Nauvoo, 9, 13, 92
Nehemiah, 3, 25
Neoclassicism, 118
Nephi, 92
Nero, Golden House of, 51, 75
New Eden, 17
New Jerusalem: John of Patmos's vision of, 9; in the Testament of Dan, 15; Eden in, 19; as a heavenly city, 27; Dante's, 38; as the model of Paradise today, 38; of the Apocalypse, 45; Milton's, 111; as the "radiant city," 144
New Testament, 19, 30
Nicholas V, Pope, 72, 74
Nichols, Stephen, 71
Niebuhr, Reinhold, 145
Noah's ark, 54
No-Stop City: A Climatic Universal City, 144
Nova Roma, 72

Odysseus, 62
Odyssey, 50, 62, 63
Orders, Vitruvian, 83
Origen, 18, 51
Ovid, 48, 51, 62

Palace, in celestial city, 14
Palace of the Sun, 63
Palatine Chapel, 72
Palladio, 98, 119
Pandaemonium, 49, 64, 65, 109
Pantheon: dedication of, as Sancta Maria ad Matryres, 71; as sacred space, 75; as a model of Paradise, 78
Paradisal motifs, 41
Paradise: literary, physical entity, 1; as garden and city, 1, 101, 103; search for, 2; definitions of, 3; mythic to metaphoric models, 8; lost, 13; Nauvoo experiment, 13; to come, 13, 19; architecture of, 14, 106; of ecstasy, 15; of serenity, 15; organic and inorganic, 17; of the past, 19; of the present, 19; after the Fall, 24; on earth, as an access, 39; of pleasure, 39, 40; as a romance, 41; antiarcadian, 46; in the Renaissance, 92; pre- and postlapsarian, 104; as a walled garden, 104
Paradise Lost, 3, 16, 44, 49, 64, 65, 101, 106–111 *passim*, 114, 135, 143
Paradiso, 38
Partonopeus de Blois, 79
Parthenia Sacra, 20
Patch, Howard Rollin, 40
Paul, Saint, 70
Paul the Silentiary, 79
Pearl, 31, 38
Pèlerinage de Charlemagne, 79
Pendentive, 78
Penshurst Place, Kent, 115
Perrault, Claude, 93
Perret, Auguste, 135
Peter, 30

Phaenomena, 48

Philip II, 83

Philippians, 30

Philo Judaeus, 3, 111

Philotheus of Pskov, 74

Phoenician temples, 26

Physics, 47

Pilgrim's Progress, 31

Planning, arcadian, 139

Plan Voisin, 135

Plat of the City of Zion, 9

Plato, 47, 49, 61, 70

Pliny, 50

Plotinus, 47

Plutarch, 123

Poetry and architecture, 17

Poggioli, Renato, 2

Pope, Alexander, 50, 82, 115, 116

Popper, Karl, 131, 143

Postmodernism, 144

Prado, Jerónimo, 83

Pre-Christian apocalyptic literature, 15

Prester John, on Paradise, 41

Priam, palace of, 64

Primitive hut, 93, 114, 118, 129, 139, 143

Procopius, 79

Proust, Marcel, 16

Psalms, 25, 26, 106

Pugin, Augustus Welby, 130

Purgatorio, 38

Pythagorean mysticism, 69

Quintilian, 16

Ragon, Michel, 46

Raphael, Archangel, 103, 107, 108, 143

Reason of Church Government, The, 145

Regia Solis. See Palace of the Sun

Republic, 47

Revelation, 15, 19, 30, 54

Romantic scientific/utopian thought, 8

Rome, 72

Rowe, Colin, 7

Ruskin, John, 16, 35, 68, 119, 130

Sacred architecture, constituents of, 54

Sacred space, 75

St. Gall, monastery of, 24

Salt Lake City, 13

Santa Croce in Gerusalemme, 71

Sant' Elia, Antonio, 135

Sant'-Ivo alla Sapienza, 92

Santo Stefano, Bologna: as Jerusalem, 75

Satan: pretensions to transcendence, 64; palace of, in heaven, 109

Scamozzi, Vincenzo, 61, 98

Seneca, 45, 47, 51, 64, 98, 114, 118, 128, 129

Sense of Form in Art, The, 132

Sforzinda, 61

Sidney, Sir Philip, 7

Silver age, 49

Simson, Otto von, 19, 139

Smith, E. Baldwin, 72, 74

Smith, Joseph: Plat of the City of Zion, 9; assassination of, 13

Socrates, 48

Sophist, 47

Space: as the essence of architecture, 75; estrangement of, 77; violation of Western concep-

Space (*continued*)
tions of, 77; as timelessness, 78
Space, Time, and Architecture, 131
Spenser, Edmund, 41
Square: as a symbol, 54; use in
Atlantis, 61
Statius, 52
Stephen, Saint, 30
Stewart, Stanley, 3
Stoicism, 52
Studio Archizoom Associati, 144
Suetonius, 75
Suger, Abbot of Saint-Denis, 70,
72
Sullivan, Louis, 123
Symbolism: of square, 54; of circle,
54, 61; of cube, 61

Tabernacle, 65
Talmud, 3, 17, 18
Tasso, Torquato, 41
Tatian, 51
Taylor, René, 53
Telemachus, 62, 63
Temple, in celestial city, 14
Temple of Solomon: as a living
creature, 26; as a microcosm of
the world, 26; rabbinical tradition, 26; destruction of, 26, 30; as
a celestial structure, 27; immaterial prototype, 27; as a celestial
prototype, 30; authority of, 53;
use of square and cube in, 54;
horn-gable in, 64; architectural
significance of, 68, 69; dimensions of, 69; transfer to city, 71;
as sacred space, 75; Hagia Sophia as a type of, 79; in Gothic
architecture, 82; reconstruction
of, 83, 92

Temples: as earth/heaven nexus,
25; Phoenician and other Middle
Eastern, 26
Testament of Dan, 15, 27
Themistocles, 44, 48
Thoreau, Henry, 123, 126, 128,
129, 130, 133
Timaeus, 61
Timelessness, 131
Timothy, 19
Trattato d'Archittetura, 93
Trissino, Giangiorgio, 98

Urban II, Pope, 72
Urban planning, utopian, 144
Utopia: Jerusalem, 2; urban plan-
ning, 144
Utopian credo, 45

Valéry, Paul, 47, 48
Vasily III, Tsar, 74
Vaughan, Henry, 24, 31
Venturi, Robert, 20
Vers une architecture, 133
Villalpando, Juan Bautista, 83, 92
Ville radieuse, 7, 131, 135, 143, 145
Viollet-le-Duc, Eugène, 130
Virgil, 16, 49, 50, 104, 115
Vitruvius, 48, 61, 82, 93, 98, 118
Vulcan (*also* Hephaestus), 64

Walden, 123, 126, 128
Walled garden, 3
Watkin, David, 131
Winter's Tale, 107, 148
Wither, George, 54, 115, 116
Wittkower, Rudolph, 82
Wölfflin, Heinrich, 132
Works and Days, 48

Wright, Frank Lloyd, 7, 50, 123, 131, 132, 133, 139, 143, 144

Yahwist fortress, 20
Yahwist garden, 3, 24

Yoch, James, 98

Zerubbabel, 68
Zeus, palace of, 62, 63

Designer: Steve Renick
Compositor: Dharma Press
Printer: Alan Lithograph, Inc.
Binder: Roswell Bookbinding
Text: 10/13 Garamond
Display: Vivaldi and Garamond